AGONY:
Brazilian Jiu Jitsu & the Ancient Greeks

Joshua Kulseth and David Larmour

Illustrated by Jeremy Smith

CANDLE LIGHT PRESS
Iowa City, Iowa

Text copyright ©2023 Joshua Kulseth and David Larmour.

Illustrations copyright ©2023 Jeremy Smith.

All Rights Reserved. This work may not be reproduced in any form without the express permission of the copyright holders (except small bits for purposes of review).

Color plates are copyright © The Trustees of the British Museum.

CANDLE LIGHT PRESS CLASSICAL is an imprint of CANDLE LIGHT PRESS.

ISBN 978-0-9895371-5-5

Book layout and edits by John Ira Thomas for Candle Light Press.

ACKNOWLEDGEMENTS

We would both like to express our profound gratitude to Cory Johnson for sharing his expertise in combat sports and his insights into ancient Greek culture, as well as for allowing us to use his classes at United Martial Arts of Lubbock as a laboratory for our ideas. His energetic support throughout, including his podcast *Grappling with the Classics*, have been critical to our success.

We would also like to thank the numerous individuals who have generously given their time and expertise to one or both of us as we worked on this project: Kodey Gulley, Jason Kocsis, Lauren Miller, Peter Miller, Marc Shumate, Josh Willms.

Joshua thanks in addition all of the coaches and teammates who have accompanied him these past seven years: without your time, expertise, encouragement, and commitment to excellence, none of this would have been possible.

Finally, we thank John Ira Thomas of Candle Light Press for preparing the book for publication and Jeremy Smith for illustrating our ideas so brilliantly in his remarkable images.

We are grateful to The Humanities Center of Texas Tech University for their generous contribution towards the cost of reproducing the images and plates in the book.

CONTENTS

RETURN TO THE PALAESTRA..................6

PART ONE: THE INITIATE AND THE AGON
The Team, The Individual, And Suffering............31
Pecking Order..................41
Sacrificial Lambs..................47
War Of Nutrition..................53
Music And Motion: The Realm Of The Muses......59
Plato Wasn't Even His Real Name..................65
Out Of The Cave..................70
A Poke In The Eye..................82
Death And Rebirth..................91
Ink..................96
The Good, The Bad, And The Stranger..................104

PLATES..................111

PART TWO: THE AGON AND THE WORLD
On The World Stage..................120
The Chimaera..................126
Centauromachy..................131
Catastrophe..................138
Spectators..................145
Trophies..................151
No Walls At Sparta..................159
The Golden Fleece..................167
The Age Of Barbarians Is Over..................175

Bibliography..................181
Endnotes..................182

PART ONE:

THE INITIATE AND THE AGON

RETURN TO THE PALAESTRA

Every city-state (*polis*) in Ancient Greece had a gymnasium and a palaestra (wrestling-school), just as most towns across the USA and many other countries today have gyms where Brazilian Jiu Jitsu and Mixed Martial Arts are practiced. Although the buildings of ancient palaestras remain only as ruins, the combat sports for which they were constructed and the principles of individual excellence (*arete*) governing these activities in Greek education, are alive and well in BJJ and MMA gyms today.[1] What follows is the story of how we discovered that when we struggle for self-improvement or victory in Brazilian Jiu Jitsu and Mixed Martial Arts today, the ancient Greeks walk among us—not only the ordinary citizens of Athens or Sparta doing their daily practice in the local palaestra but also famous athletes like Milo and Arrichion,[2] heroes of myth like Odysseus and Hercules, philosophers like Socrates and Plato, and even gods like Zeus and Prometheus.

We have called our book AGONY not only for the obvious reason, but because it includes the Greek word *agon*, meaning "struggle," "contest" and "competition" in all realms of activity—sport, political debate, legal cases, philosophical discussion, poetry, drama and other artistic endeavors.[3] The ancient Greeks were an agonistic people, devoted to the continual pursuit of excellence: as the famous line in the *Iliad* (11.784) has it, spoken by Achilles' father to his son: "always to be the best and better than all the rest." Poets and philosophers would come to the palaestra to read out or talk about their latest works, but also to wrestle. As they grappled with their fellow-citizens in the sand, they grappled with the vital questions of how best to live. Apart from wrestling, the Greeks engaged in two other combat sports, boxing and pankration—a kind of "all-in" combat, in which wrestling was combined with striking and kicking, and with limb-twisting (and -breaking) submissions, often ground-based. The pankration was named from PAN (all) and KRATOS (strength, might, power) and victory was achieved by the total immobilization, submission, or destruction of one's opponent by any and all permitted means.[4] (See PLATES 1 and 2).

The palaestra was the training-ground for combat sports, often located close to another building for athletic (and intellectual) activities, the gymnasium. The best athletes of the *polis* would periodically pit their skills in competition against their rivals from other cities at festivals in the region or indeed the whole Greek world. The most prestigious arenas were the four Pan-Hellenic festivals—the Pythia (in honor of Apollo), the Nemea (for

Zeus), the Isthmia (for Poseidon), and the greatest of all, the Olympia (held every 4 years in honor of Zeus). To be an Olympic victor—there was only one winner—was to gain "world-wide" fame, honor in one's home-city, and to move closer to the realm of the divine than ordinary mortals. In the Greek world, Time itself was reckoned by "Olympiads" the four-year intervals between each Olympic gathering.

The twofold argument we want to forward in this volume is simple and benefits from the lived experience of ourselves and others:

Firstly: the idea of competitive excellence (*arete*) in ancient Greek society, manifested in their wrestling, boxing, and pankration, is *directly* related to our contemporary culture through training and competing in modern Mixed Martial Arts, and, even more specifically, in Brazilian Jiu Jitsu.

Secondly: this notion of excellence, which so thoroughly linked athletics with all the other arts in Greek culture, is being actively rediscovered before our eyes by Brazilian Jiu Jitsu practitioners in that sport's *unique* blending of the intellectual, physical, and artistic facets of the individual personality. It happens today, moreover, regardless of class, gender, and other categories of distinction (such as free citizen vs slave) which operated in ancient Greek culture.

We will present our case with anecdotal and bio-graphical evidence as well as our on-site observations of BJJ and MMA, along with scholarly materials from archaeology, myth, literature, vase-painting and sculpture from the Greeks themselves.

The book follows Joshua's journey as an athlete and a poet—his *Odyssey* as a "fighter-poet"—through what we regard as the closest contemporary equivalent of the Greek *agon*. Along the way, we blend his personal memoir with what we believe are direct parallels with ancient Greek practices, beliefs, and myths (including Odysseus, whom we regard as the hero closest to the modern fighter we are analyzing).

These ideas have been brought to life visually in the imaginative illustrations of our graphic artist, Jeremy Smith. Short notes and a Bibliography for further reading are included. We hope that this conversation will enlighten and entertain, and most of all that it will inspire those who currently train in today's palaestras to discover a new appreciation for the beautiful and complex sport we love. To start with, though, who are we and how did we get here?

JOSHUA KULSETH

I.

I even remember the music I was listening to, practically bouncing on my feet past the 34th Street F train station on my way to the introductory class I'd scheduled with the owner of Radical MMA, located on 29th street between 7th and 8th avenues in downtown Manhattan. It was "Ophelia" by The Lumineers, and the deep resonance of the piano melody, coupled with the plucky staccato of the lead singer's voice (not to mention the excitement I felt), gave rise to a Mary Tyler Moore-type giddiness. My exhilaration and naivete was about to be hilariously contrasted with the serious, Spartan-like atmosphere of the gym I would step into in a matter of minutes, and which I'd belong to as a member for a year and a half.

One of the habits I later fostered on entering the gym, which I now heard like a cattle-call every time someone would step through the door, was the loud "OSS" we were instructed to bellow— "It means, *I will persevere through hardship*" I was told, and it became the standard response to any number of shouted instructions from the coach ("Run faster!" "OSS!" "Hip escape!" "OSS!" "See you tomorrow!" "OSS"). Throughout my conversation with the head coach, gym members would walk in, yell "OSS" and proceed to take off their shoes at the door. Never having experienced much in the way of combat sports gyms—I had started boxing at a small gym in Asheville, NC only nine months before—I was fascinated by the regimen and discipline, the adherence to a tradition, and the systematization of what seemed to me at first to be a mad amalgam of limb and muscle.

The head coach asked me about any previous injuries and experience with the sport. I told him of my short and thoroughly mediocre boxing career, followed by the honest admission of my utter helplessness on the ground—up to that point the most experience I'd had grappling was the drunken pool wrestling I'd sometimes engaged in with my buddies in Asheville. He assured me it was actually best to start from the ground level, working my way up through knowledge of positions, escapes, and submissions.

Among the many unique aspects of Radical MMA was its singular focus on a strict self-defense-based grappling program—combat Jiu Jitsu, as he called it. For my introductory lesson I learned how to close distance in a striking exchange, make contact around the waist, and take my opponent down with an inside trip. From there I was taught the basics of the mount position, striking a downed opponent, and finishing with a rear-naked choke once their back was turned. It was thrilling. I felt immediately that years of boxing knowledge and experience could instantly be negated with a simple trip, and what had been my first impression of combat sports—that of the superiority of striking over everything else—was replaced by the reality of ground fighting.

Back in Asheville, I remember asking a pro MMA fighter and former Golden Gloves champ named Kodey Gulley what his "go-to move" would be if he ever had to fight someone in the street. To my surprise he replied, *I'd double leg 'em to the concrete and choke the shit out of 'em!* I'd seen him level fighters with his infamous liver shot and watching him move in the cage was like watching a dancer, it was so artful. And here he was telling me that instead of using his striking, which was far better than mine would ever be, he'd wrestle instead. I couldn't believe it! But finding myself tripped and taken down time after time it finally clicked for me what he was talking about: there was something scarily effective about Brazilian Jiu Jitsu.

After my first lesson in grappling and humility, we came to pricing, an issue I'd run into looking at the larger, more popular gyms in the area—Renzo's, Marcelo's, Unity, etc.—whose monthly fees were completely out of the question for me, as a fresh transplant to NYC working on my Master's in Fine Arts in poetry. But I'd heard through the grapevine that this particular gym offered a bartering program to help offset the cost of tuition—for those members willing to stay on, hours after the night classes had ended, to clean the gym, it was possible to reduce the monthly cost to almost nothing. So I made a deal to stay on three nights a week and clean, which put me at only $50 a month. With a six-month membership locked in, I promised to return the following night, and did so, making it to practice an average of 4-5 nights per week for a year and a half. I was hooked.

II.

The going was anything but easy during that time. As for everyone who's started and stuck with combat sports in general, and Brazilian Jiu Jitsu in particular, the learning curve was steep. It's nothing any previous experience in sports can prepare you for (though of course some are more helpful than others—I have cross country to thank for my gas tank). The movements are too counterintuitive, the techniques too difficult to pull off during drilling, let alone in a live roll. Jiu Jitsu has been widely analogized (*it's like yoga, but involuntary; it's like fighting a shark under water*, etc.), but one of my favorites is that *it's like trying to solve a 200 lbs. Rubik's Cube that's fighting back*. Not to mention that while size, strength, and athleticism certainly play a major role later on, on day one they mean virtually nothing.

On top of the normal difficulties inherent in the sport, the gym where I spent my formative beginnings was anything but typical. Besides what I've already mentioned, the incessant *OSS*ing when entering, when leaving, when responding to the coach, as well as in your nightmares, the coach and owner ran the gym much the same way I imagine a Spartan Agoge,[5] or the old school Kodokan Judo Institute might have been run: that is, rigorously, mercilessly, and with a singular focus on excellence (think Cobra Kai—*Strike First, Strike Hard, No Mercy!*), sometimes at the expense of morale and self-esteem. There was of course no music—a staple of the more typical gyms I've been to since leaving Radical—and

it's like trying to solve a 200 lbs. Rubik's Cube that's fighting back

talking before practice was forbidden (we were told the mat space was reserved for drilling, drilling, drilling!). It wasn't unusual to be told your Jiu Jitsu sucked, nor was it unusual to spend nearly the entire class performing a single technique. During my second class I pitifully performed the standard bridge, hip-escape maneuver and was told to move over to the side of the class and repeat the movement until I'd mastered it, which, given how hopelessly uncoordinated I was starting out, took me the entire class. To the coach's credit however, there's at least two techniques I've mastered in my nearly five years of doing Jiu Jitsu: the bridge and hip-escape.

Additionally, we were strongly discouraged from consulting *Sensei YouTube* for techniques, as our coach believed in a strict hierarchy of distribution: all information poured forth from the black belt, down the ranks through brown, purple, blue, and finally to the hapless and helpless newbies, the white belts. Anything extraneous was brushed aside as *useless in a real fight.* As a result, I had no idea how to enter into even a simple open guard like Single/Full X, or Reverse De la Riva, as they were only used by the sport Jiu Jitsu types, a moniker I remember dreading (I can still hear the coach's voice, *yes, it's all well and good if you want to practice sport Jiu Jitsu, but it's not real fighting!*).

I'm sure I could fill page after page with anecdotes from the gym, but my aim is more to paint a vivid picture of the type of world I was unknowingly stepping in to, and its impact on my life and Jiu Jitsu. The coach had solid technique, and knew how to teach in such a way that the material to be covered was clearly and concisely laid out for us each class, which for anybody starting out is of the utmost importance. The new members were separated from the rest of the pack and taught the most basic fundamentals, and the advanced group separated even more from those who had mastered fundamentals, but hadn't yet gotten to the more difficult techniques and concepts. So, there was at least the feeling of being taken care of at your level, which as I've seen from my experience in other gyms, is not always the case. And even if I couldn't pull off a Berimbolo I'd secretly learned from *Sensei YouTube*, at least I had a chance of getting out of side control.

III.

And so, my life outside the gym began to adapt around what was fast becoming an enormous new obsession. During my long commutes on the subway, I'd find myself practicing gable grips on the support poles, or day-dreaming catching one of the upper belts in the Kimura I'd recently learned. Much the same way as when I'd first started boxing, I watched Jiu Jitsu matches incessantly on YouTube, and became a loyal subscriber to UFC Fight Pass. I bought Jiu Jitsu themed shirts, and even unconsciously *OSS*'d in response to my English professor's instructions (much to my embarrassment). I was all the sort of typical white belt cringe the Jiu Jitsu meming community regularly parodies.

When I wasn't in my English classes or studying, you could likely find me at the gym. I cleaned the place three nights a week (often taking several hours) with a crew of two or three guys, so I figured it made sense to train on those days as well. It was too much of a pain to haul myself back to Bed Stuy from Hunter College, so I tended to carry my gym bag along with my schoolbag with me on the train, and spent the day oscillating between campus and the gym (thank God Radical had showers—not all Jiu Jitsu joints in New York do...). Once bitten by the Jiu Jitsu bug, it held a sway over my life, and transformed me in a way which was almost entirely positive.

Growing up I wasn't physically imposing and found little outlet in the physicality I now believe is so necessary for the development of boys and young men. Instead, I retreated into my imagination, and more specifically, into the many books my school-teacher mom kept around the house. Probably like many, I was raised with the mentality then typical of contemporary American culture—that physical sports (football, baseball, boxing, etc.) are "masculine," and the arts (reading, writing, painting, etc.) are "feminine." Men and boys play sports; little girls dance or do gymnastics. So, when I didn't find my affinity in the sports I was forced into as a kid—baseball and basketball were standard, football for larger kids, and soccer was on the borderline of "sissy," in my father's words—I looked more to the arts: singing, painting, reading, and writing. Still competitive by nature, I had outlets nonetheless.

It wasn't until my late teens and early twenties that I began to discover an identity of mixed interests—in college I was an English major with a minor in poetry who hiked on weekends and played intramural sports. It was a seemingly contradictory but immensely satisfying blend I carried into my mid-to-late twenties, and into my discovery of combat sports. I realized more and more that excellence wasn't limited to traditionally masculine or feminine conceptions of one's passions. I wept over a particularly compelling performance of Shakespeare's *Coriolanus*, and exhausted myself sparring on the mats and in the ring. I wrote admittedly lame poems about boxing and Jiu Jitsu (including a haiku about the Kimura). My gym buddies and I were as apt to get together to watch Conor McGregor knock out Eddie Alvarez as we were to grab a coffee and talk about the novels of John Steinbeck.

The classes I took toward my MFA often met at night, so it wasn't unusual for me to leave the Hunter College campus on 68th and Lexington and take the subway across town to the gym on 29th. Being obsessed, I wanted to train as often as possible, but it was helpful also for blowing off steam on some nights, or simply to unwind the tension I felt in my mind after talking about poetry for three hours in a stuffy classroom. It became such a common routine that, as I mentioned before, I'd bring both my school and gym bag to class, which often prompted questions from my college classmates ("You box? That's so cool!" "What's Jiu Jitsu? Is it like karate?"). On the train home one night my professor joined me and we talked at length about the self-defense classes he'd taken three decades or so ago. After one particularly difficult semester, in a meeting with that same professor, we came to the mutual conclusion it would be far better to solve my cohort's problems by clearing the desks and having everyone fight out their difficulties rather than subject any of us to one more group discussion about feelings.

In New York especially, when I was at the peak of my physical and intellectual rigors, it felt like I was completing something in myself left unfinished by the misunderstandings, depredations, and prejudices of my childhood. I'd found a physical confidence, finally, to match the intellectual and artistic confidence I'd been fostering since high school, and I found that the Jiu Jitsu gym in particular was the special kind of environment which fostered a blending of the physical and intellectual.

IV.

Fast forward three years and a single stripe on my blue belt later, and I was in my first year of the PhD program at Texas Tech, studying comparative literature and writing poetry. I'd long left the Spartan-like combat Jiu Jitsu regimen of Radical MMA, and had discovered the wonders of the more sport-oriented techniques of Jiu Jitsu (even managing to land a Berimbolo or two on the unsuspecting white belts), as well as the dark arts of the leglock game. I'd competed in a dozen or so tournaments, and on occasion made it to the medal stand. The number of Jiu Jitsu shirts I owned grew substantially (thanks mostly to the kiosks ever-present at competitions, as well as the consolation shirts often given away with the entry fee), but I was beginning to shy away from such public displays of obsession. I'd torn my PCL, dislocated several fingers and one of my ribs (soon to be followed by another), and somehow managed more concussions than I ever had while boxing. More than ever, I was depending on my time at the gym to take my mind off the difficulties of schoolwork (the first year of the PhD is *hard*, y'all), but it was ironically within academia that one of the greatest unexpected interminglings occurred only a few weeks into my time at Texas Tech.

I'd attended a lecture on Irish poetry given by a guest speaker from Queen's University of Belfast on the Irish poet Michael Longley, and was one of the only students to raise their hands and ask what I had assumed at the time was a relatively benign question. After the talk, with my usual lack of bashfulness made bolder by years of simulating murder on the Jiu Jitsu mats, I followed up my question with others, and was asked to join the speaker, as well as her host, Dr. David Larmour, for coffee the next day.

I imagine I must have made a good impression because shortly after the pleasant coffee date with the two professors, I was told that Dr. Larmour was seeking a Research Assistant to help him along with some project or other on ancient Greek competitive culture and poetry. The details of the project mattered little to me, so I didn't ask for specifics. As a floundering first year, trying desperately to make contacts, find a mentor, and make sense of the academic career environment, this was an open door I couldn't refuse to walk through.

We made plans for a drink, and it was after the casual chatter had subsided that Dr. Larmour began filling me in on the details of his project which I had neglected to ask about. As it turned out, we had more than one shared interest. This project, a passion which had occupied him off and on for most of his professional career, but one he had not managed to complete from a lack of inside knowledge, was proving the continuity between the Greek pankration and modern MMA and BJJ. When I shared with him my own several-years-long practice of those very sports, and my love for Greek literature and culture, we were both taken aback by the striking (pun intended) coincidence. His conception for the project arose from the first version of this current volume—a comprehensive study of how the pursuit of excellence led the ancient Greeks to garner an appreciative interest in both the arts and athletics indiscriminately, an interest replicated only occasionally in our contemporary culture (one hears now and then of football players or boxers cross-training in dance or gymnastics as a way of increasing their agility and balance). We discussed how Plato divided educational training into *Mousike* (literally, "the realm of the Muses," i.e., music and the arts) and *Gymnastike* (physical training), with *Gymnastike* further subdivided into wrestling and dancing, and how he recommended that all of these activities should be practiced in contests. As we mused upon the fact that the god Apollo was honored by contests in *both* boxing and poetry, it was clear that I was just the Research Assistant he had been looking for.

DAVID LARMOUR

I.

As a newly-arrived PhD student in the Classics Department at the University of Illinois in 1982, I was assigned to assist a professor teaching Ancient Sport, a subject almost entirely unfamiliar to me. Having focused on Greek and Latin language and literature as an undergraduate, I had only the vaguest sense of what the ancient Greeks did at their Olympics or in the gymnasium. The first time I TA'ed for this class, my main duties were handing out and collecting exams, along with proctoring through the aisles in a large auditorium, and fielding student questions. My main anxiety was handling the slide projector which flashed dozens of images—statues, vase-paintings and archaeological sites—onto the giant screen on stage. As anyone over 30 will doubtless know, slide projectors were temperamental contraptions prone to all too many malfunctions: with alarming unpredictability, slides could get stuck, the carousel could stop advancing, the bulb could blow and have to be replaced. The desire to avoid embarrassment and reprimands ensured that in my first semester on duty I paid little or no attention to what Professor David Sansone was talking about. It was only later that I began to scrutinize the finely-drawn wrestlers and boxers on vase-paintings and the statues of victorious athletes in all their artistic and athletic glory. I also listened much more carefully to the professor as he talked about the funeral games held for Patroclus in Homer's *Iliad,* how Greeks wrestled (and attended talks by passing philosophers) in their gymnasiums and palaestras, and the way the competitive drive for excellence among the Greeks was embodied in the word *agon* (contest, struggle).

As it happened, this professor was also the person I soon "signed up" with as a thesis director, even though I did not yet have a clearly defined topic. I knew only that I was interested in Greek drama, especially tragedy, as, indeed, that had been the reason for coming to study with him at Illinois in the first place. One thing I had begun to notice, however, was the amazing number of images and metaphors used by the Greek tragic poets which were derived from the very sports I had been learning about in the undergraduate course for which I was his TA. When Zeus and Prometheus battled for control of the cosmos, they did so in the language of wrestling or pankration; Sophocles describes "good rivalry" among citizens as "the wrestling which is good for the city."[6] The eventual outcome was a PhD thesis on the *agon* in Greek drama and athletics—or, to put it another way, the "athletic" elements in drama and the "dramatic" elements in athletics.[7]

What I was ultimately trying to do was to narrow the gap we moderns mistakenly perceive between the two parts of Greek education, *Mousike* (poetry, singing, dancing etc.) and *Gymnastike* (physical education, training for war, fitness etc.).[8] For the Greeks these were two complementary elements within a holistic and fully unified system—Socrates says that these two arts seem to have been given to humans by a god, intending that we create a harmonious combination of *Mousike* and

Gymnastike for ourselves—and today we often we fail to recognize the full implications of this because the "artistic" and "physical" are separated in most modern educational establishments.[9] Although my study covered various sporting events—including chariot-racing—it was soon apparent to me that by far the most intriguing were the combat sports: wrestling, boxing and pankration. Unsurprisingly, these events also proved the most inspirational for poets, dramatists, painters and sculptors in Greece.

In the admittedly "sketchy" last chapter of the thesis, I speculated on how the "dramatic" features of the increasingly popular WWF professional wrestling bouts on television might be seen as somehow analogous to what went on in the ancient Greek combat arenas. I was attempting to "read" the fights as akin to dramatic dialogue, arguments between characters on stage, conflicts within a play or a poem. I was, however, simply following my nose here—I had no experience of any modern combat sport (chaotic rugby in school back in the rain-soaked grass of Ireland didn't really count) and, in the mid-80's, long before the advent of the new technologies, access to reliable sources was difficult. As a hard-working graduate student I didn't even have a television, but in my final year I spent many hours (unbeknownst to my advisor) in the University of Illinois Physical Education Library, abandoning the ancient texts of the Classics Library for journals on sports history and psychology, physical training and the like. I even managed to "interview" a few members of the Illinois wrestling team, hoping (vainly, as it turned out) for some illuminating insights.[10]

It's 1987 and I am now graduated, employed at Texas Tech University as an Assistant Professor and putting together a proposal for a new course in the Classics program there...on what else but Ancient Sport, built upon Sansone's blueprint, but which I would soon make my own, as numbers of students enrolling increased every semester, soon topping 100. It was only some years later, however, after clearing the hurdle of tenure, that I turned seriously to the task of "re-working" my thesis for eventual publication as a book. Errors were corrected, writing was tidied up, documentation was updated, and new ideas were added, and the resulting manuscript was accepted for publication in a series devoted to ancient Sport called *NIKEPHOROS*. By now, we were well into the 1990's and my "knowledge base" had benefitted from a colorful parade of students and colleagues who had strayed my way in the Texas classroom and at conferences elsewhere; I also had by now enough acquaintance with MMA, kickboxing and the UFC—then being popularized on TV and rentable videos—to at least incorporate them into some cautious comments as "worthy of further investigation." Of course, I would like to have known more about (and done more with) these sports but didn't have the means of doing so. In 1999, having completed the expected "duty" of making a scholarly monograph out of my thesis at last, I laid my Greek sporting interests aside, packed away my notes and photocopies in a large suitcase, and moved on.

II.

For well over decade following, I migrated to the world of Roman satire and the gladiatorial arena—this was of course fundamentally the same kind of "sport and poetry" study, for I had decided to show how the violent verbal sparring of the Roman satirist resembles—and is indeed inspired by—the violence on display in the Roman arena, where fighters wounded and killed each other and animal victims, just as the satirist skewers his targets on paper.[11] In the "outside world" of the 2000's, you could by now watch combat sports with ease and MMA, kickboxing and Jiu Jitsu had grown enormously in popularity—something I had certainly noticed and had even been exposed to by a "dueling duo" of Classics students who were rival practitioners in local gyms, and vocal about their adventures and skills. I never thought much, though, of my unanswered questions about the Greek *agon*, long locked away, perhaps because other duties (principally editing a well-known academic journal) prevented me from any serious engagement with these matters. I also preferred to teach Latin rather than Greek classes in those days and spent many summers in Rome and other parts of Italy. Greece and Greek sports became something of a distant memory, bathed in the nostalgic glow of a Hellenic sunset.

Then I had two significant encounters, both with a person named Joshua: first, an Honors Pre-Med. senior turned up one day at my office door asking if he could do a research project on Arrichion the ancient Greek pankratiast who expired in a competition (which he at least won, however). "What exactly do you want to look at?" I asked, with professorial suspicion. "I want to re-examine the accounts of his death from the perspective of Brazilian Jiu Jitsu," replied Joshua Willms, "because I believe I can explain what really happened." After he gave me a potted summary of his argument, I decided to take him on, and a couple of days later opened that suitcase of materials on Greek sports which had been locked away so many years before. What emerged from this foray was "An Evening of Ancient Combat Sport" where Joshua Willms explained his ingenious theory in a talk, complete with photos and diagrams, and I followed with a more pedestrian talk on aristocratic Roman volunteer gladiators who were ridiculed by satirical poets. The most striking aspect of the night, however, was the intricacy of the Brazilian Jiu Jitsu "moves" explained by Joshua and this was reflected in the detailed questions from the surprisingly large contingent of enthusiasts who turned up in the audience. I made a note to myself to find out more about this Brazilian Jiu Jitsu business.[12]

The second significant encounter happened in a chain of events started when my former undergraduate Greek professor came to campus in Fall 2019 to give a series of lectures on Homer's *Iliad* and *Odyssey*, and a public talk on the Irish poet Michael Longley's contemporary re-imaginings of these epics. At the latter event, Joshua Kulseth, a new PhD student in the poetry division of the Creative Writing program in the English Dept. asked a particularly probing question of the speaker and, after engaging in the niceties afterwards, we invited him to coffee the next day. He and the speaker had a wide-ranging discussion about Irish poetry while I sat politely on the sidelines. By this time, I had jettisoned the academic journal I was editing and finished with my gladiators, and my mind had in the meantime turned back to the Greek poets—I wanted to explore how they competed to outdo their predecessors and each other in language and imagery. It was the *agon* again, of course, but more in poetry than the realm of sport; I needed a Research Assistant well versed in poetry to help me with my investigations—and who better, I thought, than that Joshua Kulseth, who even writes his own poetry to boot? I put the offer to him over a drink a few weeks later, explaining that I was working on "the Greek poetic *agon*, not the athletic version, the *agon* in combat sports and the like, that's another story..."— to which he replied, grinning broadly and knowingly, "I can help you with *both* of those." "How do you mean?" "Well, I write and study poetry, but I practice combat sports and I compete in them too..."

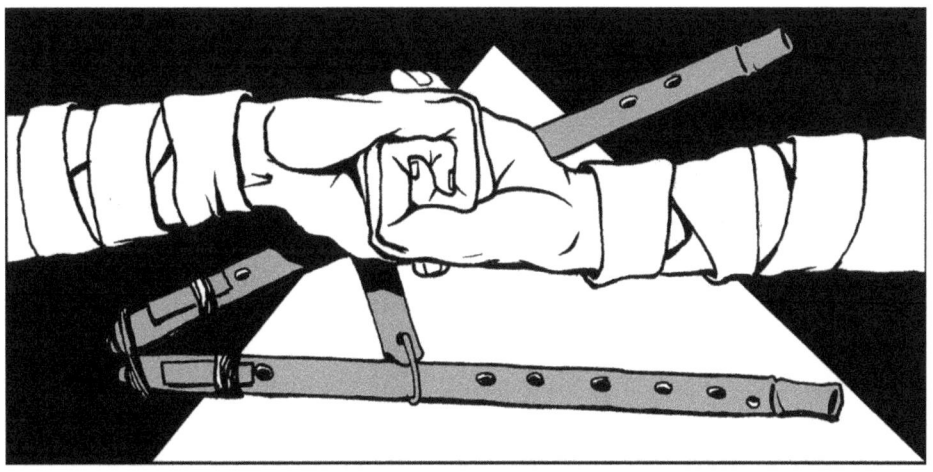

Gymnastike and Mousike

PART ONE:

THE INITIATE AND THE AGON

THE TEAM, THE INDIVIDUAL, AND SUFFERING

I played sports from the time I could hold a bat or toss a ball—as many sports as I had time for or could be forced into. From kindergarten to high school I was rounding bases, shooting free throws, scoring touchdowns, or even practicing my Ultimate Frisbee backhand. For the most part they bored me, and I stopped as soon as I had a say in the matter (somewhere around age fifteen). They were the sports I was forced to play, and I was ready to choose one for myself. And what did I end up picking? Cross-country.

I started long-distance running as a sophomore in high school, and continued through to graduation. It was the first sport where I felt like I could excel, and where the competitive bug really bit me hard. It was the first sport I felt I belonged in, where the team was one I didn't regularly feel like kicking in the ass, and one where the rewards were immediate and satisfying. And I was *fast*,

I mean *really* fast. I ran the mile in under five minutes, and the two-mile in under twelve. And perfect for a long-distance runner, I had both speed *and* a large gas tank. I could run forever. And we often did run for what felt like forever. We averaged as a team somewhere around fifty miles per week, and our varsity regularly won the state championship.

It's no surprise then, that when I found combat sports, the one thing I could rely on was my ability to go, and go, and go, and *go*. I was well-acquainted with the grind of training, and maybe even more importantly, I knew how to breathe. I could regulate my breathing, and stay calm even during the stressful and exhausting sparring rounds our boxing coach used to put us through (fifteen five-minute rounds was his favorite brand of torture). I was regularly at the front of the pack for our *Rocky* style jogging excursions around town, prompting one of my buddies, huffing and puffing after the final sprint towards the end, to grumble "Fuck your cross-country." Having excellent cardio made getting punished in the boxing ring at least somewhat redeeming, when at the end I could outlast the bigger, more muscular members of the team.

Jiu Jitsu came more easily, at least as far as cardio and long-suffering were concerned. Taking punishment is undoubtedly a characteristic of all martial arts, but nowhere is it more prolonged or intimate than in Jiu Jitsu. You could have a big dude sitting on your chest, smothering you for the entirety of a five-minute round, and the best you could do was to keep calm and try not to tap to the overwhelming pressure of it all. Add to that a sweaty Gi draped over your face and the whole experience could quickly turn horrific. Being able to breathe and stay calm was a staple of my early training (as I was frequently mounted and smashed), and the misery of running mile-repeats up and down the Ravenel Bridge in Charleston in the one-hundred-degree heat of my teenage summers had prepared me better than I could have anticipated.

Long-distance running and combat sports, besides having long-suffering in common, are equally *individual* sports, and it is the individual nature which ties back ultimately to the difficulty of training and competition. While being loosely dependent on a team effort (individual scores are added into a "team" score), these sports nevertheless depend more so than any other on a striving towards individual excellence, what the Greeks call *arete*. The team is essential—no training in running or combat could really be complete without it—but at the end of the day, in competition or otherwise, it's the individual score which matters most. The responsibility for one's performance begins and ends with one person: yourself.

Individual suffering and victory then become far more meaningful, as it isn't shared primarily with a team. Yes, a team is involved, and the importance of the team is explored elsewhere in this book, but in a hypothetical example, the skill of a Scottie Pippin would never be overshadowed by the colossal talent of a Michael Jordan. The Greeks believed likewise, and with few exceptions, the Olympic events were contests for individual glory, or *kleos*.

The Greeks had a word, *dolichos*, for a long-distance race (as opposed to a sprint or the race over two lengths of a stadium, the *diaulos*) and it implied more than its surface meaning might allude to—it concerned a particular brand of suffering: of both the body and the mind. The *diaulos* (so-named from the "double-flute" and introduced at Olympia in 724 BC, followed in the next Olympiad by the *dolichos* in 720), was an important innovation: it added the turning-post to the dynamics of the contest—a place where a runner might slip, be shoved, lose his stride, or fall as the competitors bunched together. We see here how the Greeks could refine and enhance the competition for victory in the *agon*.[13]

Dolichos means "long" or "long-lasting" and Greek vase-painters illustrated this race very differently from the sprint: the competitors are spaced further apart and running in a more relaxed style, much like Marathon racers do today. (See PLATE 3). While the sprint was one length of the stadium (190m at Olympia) and the *diaulos* was two lengths, down to the turning post and back, the *dolichos* was anywhere up to 24 lengths (over 4500m at Olympia). Victory depended not upon a sudden burst of speed but on stamina and pacing. The leader in the early or middle part of the race might well lose to someone else at the end. The *dolichos* required careful planning, more elaborate training, and deep awareness of one's own strengths and weaknesses. It was a long, hard, and carefully plotted struggle on every level.

The Greeks prided themselves on the ability to weather a superhuman amount of punishment (the Trojan War, after all, was supposed to have lasted a decade—not to mention the stories of long-suffering in *The Odyssey* and other works of ancient Greek literature), all the while keeping their wits about them and ultimately achieving victory. This principle, coupled with the individual nature of their sports, produced the culture of excellence which is the subject of this book. The names of victors at Olympia were recorded and the victory-lists survive to this day; the winners at all other athletic festivals, no matter how small and local, were also recorded (we have inscriptions from many locations), signifying the importance attached to the achievement of the individual athlete wherever Greeks lived.

In his work *Every Good Man is Free*, Philo of Alexandria discusses how the "virtuous man" fortified by the power of Reason can wear down those who use physical force and make them give up first in the struggle. To explain this better to his readers, he asks us to picture a pair of pankratiasts he once saw: one of them (who is the equivalent of the man of Force) landed all his well-placed punches and kicks and thus "did absolutely everything required to achieve victory" in the match, but nevertheless left the arena "in a state of complete exhaustion" and thus lost. How did this come about? Philo describes his opponent ("the one who is hit," the equivalent of the man of Reason) as follows: "a mass of densely-packed flesh, taut, hard and solid, packed with athletic spirit, with sinews all strained, like rock or iron" and says that he thus "broke down the power of his adversary for a total victory."[14]

That concept, *dolichos*, could easily be applied to Jiu Jitsu. In what other sport or activity does a lengthy physical and mental exertion more clearly manifest itself? The suffering is immediate and prolonged, and doesn't abate as one advances in skill, as there are always more obstacles and trials to test oneself against ("There's always a bigger fish…"). The individual nature of Jiu Jitsu, coupled with one's ability to suffer long and well, allow for a greater renown, discipline, and self-satisfaction than those sports which are based around a team.

One of the reasons I was attracted to the no-time-limit types of tournaments (dubbed "submission only" for obvious reasons) when I first started training Jiu Jitsu was precisely because it lent itself to the same type of long-distance running mentality I had fostered for years, i.e. the race is going to be a long one, so there's no need to burn yourself out at the starting line. I could take my time on the feet if I wanted to, practicing takedowns I wouldn't be as apt to risk if points were at stake, or I could sit guard and work out some new open guard technique I'd been drilling recently. The world was my oyster as long as I didn't give up the submission, which, since my first gym focused intensely on teaching escapes, I wasn't too worried about. I had the endurance to take the fight into deep waters, regularly surpassing half an hour, forty-five minutes, and even the hour mark occasionally. If my opponent couldn't keep up then time was on my side; if he could, then when exactly would be my breaking point? The Greeks had a similar mentality. Fights had no time limits, and only the fighters could decide when the show ended. Like our modern-day "tap," the Greek athletes who wished to concede defeat had only to lift a finger and it was all over. (See PLATE 2). While I think there are virtues in both modes of competition (points vs. submission only), I do believe in the purity of a no time limit, no point contest—when only the sheer grit and skill of an athlete determines victory.

At the same time, contrasted with the inherent individuality of the sport, one of the peculiarities of Jiu Jitsu, more so than in wrestling or boxing, is an obsession with martial lineage as a means of validating the quality of technique. Walking into Radical MMA for my introductory class I noticed something which wasn't there at my previous gym (which was dedicated primarily to boxing and wrestling): on the walls were hanging pictures of old men in Gis, rowed in what seemed like an order of progression. The most common in Jiu Jitsu circles, as I learned later, was a portrait of Helio Gracie, one of the founders of Brazilian Jiu Jitsu. After him in popularity followed Mitsuyo Maeda (instructor of the Gracies), and even Jigoro Kano (the founder of Judo). Pictures of other masters, whether another one of the Gracies, or popular figures, as well as the black belt operating the gym itself, might also be present. At Radical, Bruce Lee, along with one of his inspirational quotes, greeted students at the top of the stairs leading down to the matted space where we had classes.

It's a practice inherited from Jiu Jitsu's Judo legacy, and from its traditional placement as a "martial art." The legitimacy of one's belt color often depends on lineage, and whether or not the inherited technique is "up to snuff" so to speak. Considering a black belt in Jiu Jitsu can take, on average, ten years to achieve, the preoccupation with lineage isn't without some legitimacy. After all, who wants to spend a decade or more of their lives getting a black belt only to get wrecked by an over-eager blue belt, the kind of wake-up call many of us would have trouble handling?

Techniques, too, have their roots in lineage. Perhaps most famously, the figure-four lock known as the Kimura takes its name from the Japanese judoka Masahiko Kimura, who used it to devastating effect in his controversial match with Helio Gracie. At Radical MMA we had the "Jake Shields Guillotine" (an arm-in guillotine from full guard, named after MMA fighter Jake Shields), the "Jacare Pass" (a butterfly-guard pass, named after world champion Ronaldo "Jacare" Souza), and the "Rat Guard" (an invention of our coach, Rene Dreifuss, whose nickname was "the rat"). I could easily fill the rest of the chapter with other examples.

If one were to time-travel to the 5th century BC and walk into a Greek palaestra, one obviously wouldn't find posters of Helio Gracie or Mitsuyo Maeda, but one would find likenesses of the demi-god Hercules, an athlete or coach of local renown, or poets such as Pindar and Corinna famous for singing the praises of athletes and placing them in the company of the heroes of myth. Pindar and Corinna were themselves rivals in an *agon* of poetry.[15] Lineage shaped not only Greek athletics, but their entire culture, the heroic legacies of leading citizens serving as inspiration and examples for an entire city-state. Legacy was the lifeblood of their society and the glory of the victor who had triumphed at Olympia or another Panhellenic festival would enhance the reputation of the polis he lived in. The Greek poet Pindar is a prime example of how this operates. In his victory-odes to famous athletic victors at the four great Panhellenic festivals (Olympia, Delphi, Nemea and Isthmia) he frequently spends far less time praising the feats of the individual in question (let alone describing the contest itself, which he barely touches upon) than he does the lineage of the athlete and achievements of his forebears. Famous heroes like Hercules or Theseus are often invoked alongside the victor's family line. In Pindar's victory odes (called *epinikia*), victory (*nike*) in the contest becomes a communal accomplishment, bringing glory or shame to family and city-state. A good example is provided by his *Olympian Ode* 8, commissioned to celebrate the victory of Alcimedon of Aegina, in the Boys' Wrestling in 460 BC. He defeated all comers at the Olympia, but Pindar takes time to praise Alcimedon's brother Timosthenes for his victory at the Nemea and the trainer Melesias who had himself won the crown in the pankration— "it's easier for someone who has knowledge from his own experience to teach others." Finally, he observes that Melesias has been honored by a 30th victory won for him by Alcimedon, who (in the fine old translation by Wheelright):[16]

> "With fortune and his manly arm to aid,
> He sent four vanquish'd striplings back in shame,
> Darken'd their homeward path with sorrow's shade,
> And gave to slandering infamy their name."

This triumph, Pindar adds, also breathed into Alcimedon's grandfather "the vigor that wrestles against old age" for "Hades is forgotten by the man who possesses great accomplishments." The point is that Alcimedon's victory re-invigorates his aging grandfather because it means his name will now live on after death.

As a competitor I've found, more so than individual glory, my thoughts pre-tournament fixate around my coach and teammates: "please don't let me embarrass myself in front of my team" or "just let me make my coach proud" are frequently on my mind as I velcro the blue or red strap around my ankle and step into my match. Winning is great, but showing the world (or at least the spectators huddled around my numbered mat) the legitimacy of my gym's technique is often my greater concern. Olympic athletes humiliated by defeat in the 5th century BC were not welcomed by the sound of "sweet laughter" when they returned to their mothers, as Pindar says in another poem (*Pythian Ode* 8, for Aristomenes of Aegina, victor in wrestling), but "slunk home along back roads, avoiding the eyes of their enemies, gnawed by their misfortune." The modern Jiu Jitsu competitor, while benefitting from the inclusion of 2nd and 3rd place medals (an indulgence not usually available to the Greeks outside some competitions in democratic Athens), nevertheless might still feel the sting of a loss most when sulking back to his or her team waiting on the sidelines.[17]

PECKING ORDER

In Asheville, NC, I belonged to a particularly rowdy Jiu Jitsu gym. We called it "The Mountain Division" and took pride in our ability to endure and dole out grueling punishments. We heel-hooked in the Gi (white belts included), we regularly drilled slicers and cranks, and we even innovated a particularly nasty toe hold dubbed "The Ringworm" (Q: "Why is it called The Ringworm? A: "Because it's shitty"). It was, and still is, the wild west of Jiu Jitsu: anything goes, so long as you're willing to accept the repercussions for your cheekiness.

With that comes a certain understanding of who's most likely to put you through the most pain, and who you can get away with practicing shenanigans on. Thinking of falling back for a heel-hook on the coach, I'd better be ready for the fury of his catch-wrestling. Am I willing to grind my head against my opponent's face in order to break out of mount and potentially risk a worse reversal? These are the thoughts running through your head as you roll in "The Mountain Division." On the one hand it may seem harsh: our numbers are purposefully small, and we put new guys through the ringer. On the other hand, I believe it's ultimately desirable for its equity: I can take the same risks with the day-one-new-guy as I can with the twenty-year-black-belt. If I manage to submit the coach, then bully for me—he'll smile and nod and maybe even grunt congratulations—but I'd better be ready for a fight in the next round. When the rules and pecking order are clear, it might be harsh, but it's still fair.

And that brings me to the point: what's a pecking order, and why does it matter in Jiu Jitsu gyms? The term "pecking order" comes from our understanding of the social hierarchy of chickens (who's going to be able to peck for food, and when). The connection to the social dynamics in a Jiu Jitsu gym is perhaps clear from my brief explanation, but unless you've been on the mats for a while, the practical aspects of that dynamic are difficult to determine, and not obvious to the outsider.

In a well-functioning gym, a pecking order provides a guidepost by which a newcomer might gauge their abilities and strive to climb the ranks. It isn't dependent on the color of your belt, but your skill level, which of course makes receiving a higher belt more meaningful—if you're a blue belt or higher, you know in your bones that you had to earn it. It's a pure meritocracy on the Greek model. As a result, lower belt ranks have no need to shy away from challenging higher belts, or even the coach, so long as they're willing to take a beating if they fail.

And we do fail, often. But in addition to the equality a clear pecking-order provides, it gives weight to the mile-marker achievements in one's journey. I'll give you an example. At "The Mountain Division" I have a Jiu Jitsu antagonist, a competitive rival, a frienenemy, if you will. His name's Marc, and he's been practicing Jiu Jitsu for about a year and a half longer than me. When we first rolled, we immediately clicked. This happens sometimes with your "favorite" training partner, the one who just "gets" you, and can reciprocate in a way that pushes you to work harder, all the while accommodating your body

type and style. Marc and I have violent rolls; we give no quarter, and we ask none. Ironically, Marc and I have never injured each other (in spite of our many attempts), which attests to the positive dynamic between us. Marc is a notch or two above my own skill level, and I make no bones about it. In fact, Marc is my own milestone for improvement. We have a running ratio of submissions—I submit Marc once for every eight or nine times he submits me, and we've maintained this ratio pretty much since first rolling. I feel no animosity about my lower place in the pecking order, nor does he overly exert his position outside of sparring. We maintain an equilibrium from our understanding of our respective statuses in the gym. And this isn't unique to the two of us, but is the case with everyone in that gym. The atmosphere of equality and competition ranks members according to merit rather than the supposed esteem garnered by their belt color or time spent on the mats.

We know very little about the concept of a pecking order in the palaestras of ancient Greece, but we can ascertain from evidence of their rules and practices that it was as close to a meritocracy as existed in the ancient or contemporary world. The world of wrestling and pankration were, firstly, only open to all male Greek citizens, which from the outset establishes an ordered equality (even if that "equality" is inherently exclusionary from a modern perspective). Secondly, there were no weight classes in either practice or competition. While this might seem at first glance to be an example of natural exclusion (the stronger man will almost always trounce the smaller), it nevertheless confirms the largely indiscriminate nature of ancient gym practices and competitions. There were age-divisions—youths and men—which went some way towards regulating size and musculature, but only partly.

Rather than separate variously sized men, the rules of the palaestra allowed for the possibility that a smaller man might use his natural abilities to triumph over the larger, thus increasing their esteem in the community and place in the pecking order. Thirdly, there were no distinctions of skill level when arranging the training or competing order. The novice and expert alike pitted their strength, skill, and wits in the sand, and the possibility for glory was thereby undiminished. Lastly, we have reason to believe that the training in the palaestra was at the very least an indirect preparation for the rigors of warfare, and as a result, fostered an all-pervasive sense of community and dependence which the Greeks believed only a meritocracy could instill. The man in the front lines could be assured of the reliability and skill of the men to his left and right; he could be assured the same men who strove so arduously with him in the gym and in competition could equally be depended on to stand firm with him in battle.

A clear and fair pecking order builds trust in the gym, prevents intentional injuries, improves the collective skills of the group (each member being unafraid to try new or risky techniques), and provides a sense of pride and accomplishment as one progresses in skill. Brazilian Jiu Jitsu, more than any other martial art, is a "fuck around and find out" type of sport, but a merit-based pecking order makes it enjoyable to "fuck around," and safe to "find out."

SACRIFICIAL LAMBS

Everyone remembers what it was like getting pounded on as a white belt, but thankfully for those poor souls still wrapped in that particular belt, it won't become apparent just how terrible the beatings were (or how bad your technique was), until after you've been promoted. It's an interesting fog-of-war, being a newbie, and thank the gods too, because if we knew just how hopeless we all were at the start there'd be no higher belts. And yet this phase of learning—or perhaps being learned *upon*, since you're mostly just fodder for the upper belts—is indispensable, for those just beginning as well as all the upper belts. Since it's impossible to jump to a higher belt without the grind of starting out, there'd literally be no Jiu Jitsu without the men and women on the bottom of the totem pole. Likewise, without those meat-puppets to practice on, the higher belts would have no effective means of incorporating new techniques during live rolls, since experimenting on blue belts or higher becomes significantly more difficult as they have some idea of what the hell they're doing. Much like the animal, or even the occasional human sacrifices of the ancient world, these victims serve a crucial purpose for the functioning of a society (in this case, the society of a gym). Popular memes and sayings emerge from this reality—"A Black Belt is a White belt who never quit," "White Belts are Friends not Food," "Jiu Jitsu people just be bored watching a murder," and so on.

Let's talk about sacrifice. No doubt many of us are familiar with the sacrificial practices of ancient civilizations, if only from Sunday school or vague memories of world history classes in high school. The gist of the system is this: the gods have made us, blessed us with sustenance, and demand a level of propitiation for their efforts, namely, sacrifices—usually in the form of an unblemished animal, a white lamb being the most archetypal. Of course, the ancient Greeks were no different, and we often read of the failure to offer sacrifice as the main reason behind the gods' wrath against particular individuals or groups. Likewise, the promise of sacrifice could mean the difference between victory or defeat in armed conflict (think of any number of battle-vows made in the *Iliad*).

But why *unblemished* animals? We might think back to *Genesis*, when God delights in the first fruits of Adam's son Abel, while taking issue with Cain's likely second-rate sacrifice—divinities demand of their creatures the very best, the purest of their fruits and flocks, to more thoroughly measure their devotion. After all, who wouldn't like to keep the best for themselves? But to sacrifice it proves a commitment to the specific communal deity all the more. Seems logical enough through that lens. Prizes at the four Panhellenic festivals were richly symbolic of the link between the human and divine realms: the athlete was crowned with a wreath of leaves from the sacred plant of the presiding deity (so of olive leaves at Olympia for Zeus, laurel at Delphi for Apollo). The victor also had red or white ribbons (similar to those adorning a sacrificial animal) tied around his thigh, upper arm and forehead, symbolizing his dedication to the god of the contests and his distinguishing from all the rest as the supreme athlete in the particular event.

There are different kinds of sacrifices though, more so than just a giving of one's first-fruits. There's also a sacrifice of purification as reparation for one's individual sins, or the sins of the community. This type of sacrifice is largely what I'm driving at when I make the connection between the ancient world and our contemporary combat culture. And it's this ritual in which discussion of the *purity* of the sacrifice becomes more relevant, as the degree of an animal's purity was directly related to the level of appeasement. Perhaps you can guess what I'm driving at now. While we no longer slaughter animals on the altar in honor of the gods or in atonement for our sins, we still practice a type of sacrifice in our combat culture—the ritual killing of white belts on the altar of violence, the mats.

Now, it's certainly not always as melodramatic as that, but hear me out. Earlier I talked about the indispensability of white belts in the gym, and of their essential role in the support of higher belts (not to mention the financial needs of the owners), so it seems of some merit to analogize their role as sacrifice. After all, let's look at the color of their belt—*white*, a conventional sign of purity (and inexperience). And who hasn't at one time or another looked at white belts with the condescending *bless your heart* pity stare; the same one you might use for a misbehaving child caught with its hand in the cookie jar or golden retriever caught in the act of chewing a favorite loafer. Furthermore, it's generally understood that the act of tapping out is symbolic of death; of saying all right, you've killed me. It's no stretch of the imagination then to relate the frequent (and I mean very frequent) tapping out of white belts to the purifying sacrifice of a slaughtered lamb.

But the connections don't stop merely with the color of the belt, or even with white belts in general. It's worth shifting focus for a moment to the emergence of the UFC as a popular source of combat entertainment, and as a kind of litmus test for the developing technique of the combat sports community. For anyone who's ever watched the early UFC events, they were a mess—entertaining no doubt, but a mess. Between the single-gloved Art Jimmerson, the roided-out Ken Shamrock sporting a banana hammock, Teila Tuli the former Sumo star, or Royce Gracie managing to beat them all while wearing pajamas, it seemed like a parody of the 1988 Jean-Claude Van Damme blockbuster *Bloodsport*. Nevertheless, it was the first and closest thing we had at the time to a no holds barred fighting sport—the Greek pankration in effect—and quickly developed into a legitimate combat entertainment business.

But between then and now a number of lesser-skilled fighters were sacrificed for the sake of a developing industry. One thinks of the early brawling bout of Forrest Griffin and Stephan Bonnar, which is credited as sparking the UFC's first real popular success. There was no shortage of heart (what the Greeks would call *thumos* or *menos*)[18] in the two fighters, but little visible technique outside of wild swinging fists. It was bloody, brutal, and immensely entertaining. No doubt it would be of equal interest to the concussion expert as to the casual combat sports fan. But it was a necessary sacrifice for the sake of the sport, and it wasn't made by those two alone, but by any number of fighters swinging for the fences against other equally brutal bruisers (one thinks of Quinton "Rampage" Jackson, Chuck "The Iceman" Liddell, Wanderlei "The Axe Murderer" Silva, and many others). There are few, if any, of the Old Guard left, and even fewer devotees of their fighting style. Most of today's top fighters are crisp, technical, and trained to avoid damage as much as they are to inflict it. As I'll argue in a later chapter, the age of the barbarians is over.

Likewise, the age of the sacrificial lamb (in the UFC at least) is over as well. Though there are still remnants: observe for instance the color of the Octagon mat— white. It's no coincidence, as a white mat is the best color for displaying the bloodstains of fighters, and as the fights progress, the mat grows ever redder, culminating in the headlining match, after which the mat is either cleaned or thrown out. The Octagon is a kind of sacrificial altar on which is drained the life of fighters, to lesser or greater degrees, for the sake of both their own careers and the perpetual existence of the sport. When the blood stops flowing, the death of the sport is soon to follow.[19]

Returning to the white belt in Brazilian Jiu Jitsu, it's important to note the inherently temporary nature of the rank. When one is a white belt, one is sacrificing not only for the sake of the higher belts and the gym, but also for one's own progress. The hope is then to progress from being the one put under the knife to the one holding the knife, so to speak. And this is where the analogy naturally concludes, as it certainly involves "death," but more so it sustains and perpetuates the life of combat sports in our contemporary culture.

WAR OF NUTRITION

Before I started boxing at the age of 24, my idea of nutritional awareness was abstaining from eating an entire pizza by myself in one sitting, either saving some for others, or myself later. My health-conscious friends would often roll their eyes at my indiscriminate diet and seemingly iron-clad digestive system. But hey, I was still "relatively" skinny after years of pizza and beer, and in good enough shape to competitively play a full day's worth of ultimate frisbee or go for a long run, so what did it matter to me? As long as I still looked good naked and could stay active, nutrition was as far out of my mind as setting up a 401k or getting a colonoscopy.

Along with this nutritional ignorance was a general ignorance of my own body. I knew from years of cross country running how to address some basic injuries like muscle cramps, shin splints, or the occasional bruised heel, but besides that very limited "expertise" I was oblivious of how my body worked. And to be honest, I didn't really care. If it ain't broke, don't fix it... or think about it at all for that matter.

But combat sports has always been a peripheral interest of mine, and so when I finally jumped in, my first confrontation wasn't with an opponent's gloves in my face, but with the limitations of my body under the stress of exertion. It seemed to me boxing required the full attention of my body—I couldn't just put it on autopilot for 8 miles or so like I could when I was running—it combined all the rigors of cross country with the newfound intensity of near-constant "fight or flight" sensory engagement. In practice I had to survive fifteen rounds of my cardio working over-time while also managing to keep my wits about me as I fought for my life.

The first thing that needed trimming was my waistline. While I was still technically a skinny guy, my love handles had grown slightly more handly over the years, and I needed to shed the fat and put on some muscle. Secondly, in order to continue to survive the onslaught of sparring partners every practice (or even just the rigors of our gym's intensive bag work), I needed to figure out how to be as healthy as possible to offset the discomfort of the workout. That's where nutrition came in. I overhauled my diet—began eating greens of some kind every day, taking multi-vitamins, eating less, and most importantly of all, eating clean. I laid off the booze and adapted my diet and, surprise! What a difference it made. Though my skills left a lot to be desired, I was at least able to survive the rounds without getting too winded or (a normal occurrence) blowing chunks in the parking lot. Pretty soon I'd lost around 25lbs and could throw at least a nominally intimidating jab.

Picking up Brazilian Jiu Jitsu nine months later increased my bodily awareness exponentially. No longer could I stave off my opponent with a half-decent jab; the work only *began* once the two of us were locked together. And if I thought I was engaging new muscles in boxing, Jiu Jitsu was an even ruder awakening. Everything was sore, or hurt, *all the time.* In my first few weeks I bruised my ribs, and could barely swallow food for all the choking I'd endured. The "gentle art" was not so gentle, as I'd come to find out. But with the problem of injuries came the solution of fixing them; with my newfound bodily awareness, as well as the guidance of some more knowledgeable friends, there wasn't any injury I couldn't seem to treat on my own. I could even prevent future injuries with the administration of a handful of exercises and a modicum of weight-lifting. Coupled with a continually growing knowledge of nutrition, combat sports had equipped me with a means for knowing my body, both physically and mentally.

What I come to now is an understanding of the competitive space (what we've called the *agon*) as a basic zone of experience and awareness. That experience and awareness begins physically, with the body's adjustment to the new practices and challenges, and moves from there into the mental space of toughness and perseverance—learning to master the groans of your body with the discipline of your mind. In a way, the gym shows you who are really are, and what you're capable of— "the mat is the truth," as Kazushi Sakuraba once put it.

This isn't a new concept—ever as we're "discovering" it, the ancient Greeks had long ago pinpointed the importance of these disciplines and the accompanying care and attention needed by the body active in its practice of them. The bodies of athletes were often thoroughly massaged by a specialist (*paidotribes*) using olive oil. Diet was strictly regulated, especially for the elite athletes, by coaches, and each diet was tailored to their need. Greek athletes competed naked, a surprising notion to modern Western imaginations, but a practice nonetheless which indicates an extraordinary respect, even reverence, for the human body. Indeed, before they went out to compete under the blazing sun at the Olympia, for example, their bodies would be smeared in olive oil and acquire a "heroic gleam" as they emerged into the agonal space. This reverence is also captured by Greek sculpture, which displays in the minutest detail the sinews of bulging muscles, the intricacy of veins, and even the precise location of wounds received in competition.[20]

There is an important parallel between the athletes displayed in Classical Greek art, and those practicing and competing today: facial expression (or, rather, the lack of one). Though I'm no gambler, I have managed to acquire a formidable poker face (if only I were any good at poker), which I frequently use on the mats. Hiding emotions from your opponent, especially when they've landed a particularly hard blow, or transitioned to a dominant position, is essential for anyone who wants to compete in combat sports. Some might even argue it's essential for a healthy inter-gym competitiveness too. But this poker face, so to speak, is only perfected with practice, as one becomes more aware of one's body, especially under extreme stress. I know what a punch feels like, so when I get hit in the face for the 1045th time, it comes as no surprise that it hurts. As a result, I'm better able to mask that hurt with my neutral facial expressions (and maybe learn to bob and weave occasionally). This is what I like to call a cultivation of calm, and it begins with breathing. Learning how to breathe properly is important for everything from proper sleep to competing in the ADCC's, and nowhere is it better taught than in the sink-or-swim combat sports environment. Even the most physiologically inept will, if they continue to strike or grapple, have to learn how to control their breathing. If they don't, they will always be the guy who gets beat up, and will likely quit sooner or later.

   This cultivation of calm, and its outward sign in a neutral facial expression, is just as common in Greek athletic sculpture as the nakedness of its figures. Neutral expressions which, if you pay attention, you'll find plastered on most of the high-to-elite level combat athletes today. It's a calm which, for the Greeks, was useful not only for their Olympic games, but also for the frequent warfare they engaged in. More relevantly for us, for the average Jiu Jitero or boxer, claiming no stake in the ADCCs or WBA Championship belt, the physiological knowledge and cultivation of calm allows for the managing of one's body under stressful circumstances, either professional or social. If I were to, hypothetically speaking, rear-end a car in a coffee shop parking lot, or more commonly, if I have to present my academic papers and creative writing at conferences, combat sports have given me the ability to control the inevitable adrenaline rush I experience through breathing exercises and mental toughness. I reason to myself before a big class presentation, "Well, at least I'm not getting punched in the face," or in an uncomfortable social situation, "At least no one is trying to strangle me," and before long, the stress of the situation fades into an assured self-control. Consistently facing the stress and fear of training in the gym makes living the rest of my life seem like a springtime stroll through the park.

MUSIC AND MOTION: THE REALM OF THE MUSES

The Greeks understood the importance of music in training, even if they hadn't yet discovered the 808 or auto-tune. Practices and matches were often accompanied by the *diaulos* (double-flute), which we have evidence for in many training scenes on vases, depicting javelin-throwers, long-jumpers and boxers. (See PLATE 4). Music was used to inspire and keep time, as well as to entertain. Indeed, for the Greeks, music and movement went closely together: dance was intimately connected with both athletics and physical training for warfare. We hear in the Athenian Panathenaic festival of a Pyrrhic dance, said to have been invented by Athena to celebrate the defeat of the Giants by Zeus and the Olympian gods—an *agon* for control of the cosmos. Teams of dancers with weaponry would compete in a display of movements with spears and shields, and these teams would be classified according to age groups, as in other athletic competitions. These teams have a close parallel in the singing choruses that would compete in poetic competitions, and also in the theatrical chorus which danced and sang its lines in every Greek tragedy or comic drama. Rhythmic and synchronized movement and sound were presumably the most important skills—that is, harmony in everything, mind and body.

A modern Jiu Jitsu or MMA gym without music playing in the background or punctuating rounds of hard-sparring is like a house without walls or a body without a heartbeat—it's bare, uninspired, dead. A gym's music is the pulse, the rhythm, of the entire body where the work of training is being done. It hammers out a beat with its pace, and inspires with its lyrics. In short, it's hard to imagine the kind of uninhabited place its absence would express. Interestingly, the Jiu Jitsu gym where I trained in NYC was exactly that kind of place—bare of distraction, it was at times equally bare of inspiration.

Descending to the training basement of such a building was like entering into another world: a 19th century Japanese Judo dojo, perhaps. And the sparsity of music, posters, or other accoutrements accompanied the conviction that training should be rigorously focused and uninterrupted by distraction. It was a serious place which, on the one hand, certainly facilitated a heightened level of attention (especially helpful for drilling new positions), but on the other, contributed to a misplaced sense of loyalty, and a mechanical adherence to technique.

By misplaced sense of loyalty, I'm referring here to the dangerous susceptibility of martial arts gyms to becoming a cult of personality. This is nothing new, for as long as there have been specialists willing to offer their trade to the public, there have been people willing to go to great lengths to learn from them. Jiu Jitsu and MMA gyms are especially notorious for this. I've had friends who uprooted their lives—jobs, relationships, homes—in order to train with a Marcelo Garcia or John Danaher. And there's certainly nothing wrong with that, so long as there are mechanisms within those gyms for dispersing authority and disseminating information. One of those mechanisms is the use of music in training. Without music, the silent gap is liable to be filled instead with the most dominant personality in the room, typically the head coach. Instead of the raucous sounds of T-Pain, DMX, or Metallica, the voice of the coach instructing students is all that's heard in between grunts or deep breaths.

What this does to the atmosphere and psychology of a gym, and of its individual members, is maybe becoming clearer. Instead of allowing the gym members to enter into themselves (which music often does) in order to find the drive and inspiration to improve or persevere, it's only ever the voice of the instructor in their heads. Gradually, any individual self-expression is superseded by the will of that dominant personality, and a check on the power of their influence is eliminated. The loyalty which one owes to oneself, to one's progress, to one's mental health, is instead replaced with the unhealthy cultish loyalty these environments can engender (whether purposefully or not). Loyalty to one's gym—one's teammates and coaches— is a perfectly natural aspect of training, but when that loyalty is untempered by reality, by outside voices and rhythms, then too often a gym can become a toxic training environment, regardless of the level of skill of the instructor. The ancient Greek scholar Philostratus (whose book *Gymnastike* we will cite frequently) tells several anecdotes about the excesses of trainers, including one who killed his athlete by forcing him to train as usual when he was suffering from indigestion.[21]

Okay, but what do I mean by a mechanical adherence to technique, and how does the absence or presence of music affect it? No doubt anyone training martial arts long enough has suffered technique fatigue—the boredom which inevitably follows a general familiarity with a technique or series of techniques. Without a steady thrumming of music in the background of a training session, filling the space with an emotional rhythm, drilling technique is likely to become stale and uninspired. And don't be confused by the term "emotional rhythm," as it just means the emotional temperature of the room, established by a number of factors—the head coach, your training partners, the general attitude of each member, the layout of the gym, and the music playing in the background.

Think of emotional rhythm like the soundtrack to a good television show, but more specifically, the theme song. Each show has its own unique introduction, from the immediate "So no one told me life was gonna be this way" *clap clap clap* of *Friends*, to the gritty "Red Right Hand" of *Peaky Blinders*, to the parting clouds and fast-paced register of *The Simpsons*. A television show's trademark is its theme song, recognizable even to those who've barely watched the show. The song becomes a shorthand for the emotional imprint that particular show leaves on the minds of its viewers. Likewise, a gym has its own emotional imprint (or rhythm) dictated by those factors, but especially the music choice—which is generally consistent and chosen by the head coach. While everyone's tastes may differ, and each gym may have its own particular musical aesthetic, an established rhythm is essential in the combat training environment, as it not only focuses the mind, but inspires within the gym community an *esprit de corps* responsible for its continued success.

It's no groundbreaking notion that music can have an impact on our emotions: we listen to sad music when we're sad, and it makes us sadder; we listen to happy music when we're happy and it makes us even happier, etc…and we begin to associate certain songs with our emotional states or life circumstances when we first listened to them. I vividly remember sitting lovesick on a bus in the 8th grade listening to The Red Hot Chili Peppers' "Soul to Squeeze" on repeat as our class left the Six Flags parking lot. So, too, can I remember the remixed Lil Wayne tracks I used to pump me up on the day I won my first double gold at a Jiu Jitsu tournament. Music has a power over our minds, and that power can be harnessed in the gym to form neural pathways which increase the likelihood of technique retention, as well as enhancing the general pleasure of our classes.

Returning to the mechanical adherence to technique, a music-less gym, like a body without a soul, is more likely to result in unimaginative rolling styles. Not only will boredom imprint on our rote execution of technique, but it will severely limit our *enjoyment* of the sport and therefore our willingness to engage in adventurous rolling. Music, giving rhythm and inspiration to the mind and body, can stimulate in our technique a spirit of experimentation, leading to a substantially more enjoyable experience rolling, as well as an increased likelihood that our Jiu Jitsu game will grow and improve as we test the boundaries of our ability.

No discussion of music and rhythm would be complete without mentioning its inherent connection to dance and movement. When he was still a child, and before he was allowed to train as a boxer, Vasyl Lomachenko's father enrolled him in dance classes and gymnastics, demanding a level of excellence in the arts of movement and flexibility before permitting him to begin his combat training. To ancient Greeks, this would be perfectly normal. Athenaeus says that "positions were carried over from choral dances into the wrestling-schools" and, he adds, young Greeks would "learn courage through music and athletic training" which in turn led to exercising in armor to musical accompaniment (as with the Pyrrhic dance mentioned above).[22] And as we know, Lomachenko went on to become one of the most accomplished amateur boxers of all time (with a record of 396 wins and 1 loss) before entering into a long and decorated professional career. A virtuoso of movement and precision in the ring, Lomachenko's enormous success as a fighter is due in large part to his grounding in dance and gymnastics. In a word, it's his superior *rhythm* which distinguishes him from his peers.

Ask any fighter with any amount of experience on the mats or in the ring, and of all the qualities important for success in their sport, good *timing* will no doubt be among the top answers. When the levels of strength and technique are similar, it's the fighter with superior timing who will win the day. And timing is rhythmic, and thus musical in nature. When we watch BJJ and MMA, especially when performed by masters of the art, we are watching an intricate dance on the Greek model.

PLATO WASN'T EVEN HIS REAL NAME

When I was a freshman in college, I read Plato's *Republic* for the first time in an *Intro to Philosophy* class. Not mentioned of course in the book was a nifty factoid I managed to keep stored somewhere at the back of my brain for years before realizing how interesting it really was: Plato wasn't even his real name—*Platon,* which is derived from the Greek *platys,* meaning "broad," was a nickname given to him by his wrestling coach, Ariston of Argos, because of the breadth of his chest and shoulders.[23] Plato, one of the most famous philosophers in history, was not only an accomplished wrestler (said to have competed at the Isthmian Games), but was proud enough of his athletic accomplishments to adopt his own moniker to the point that his real name (Aristocles, by the way), has been almost completely forgotten.

The idea that a philosopher like Plato, who enjoyed singing and writing poetry, and was often portrayed as grey-bearded and old, could also kick the shit out of you, was mind-blowing to me, having grown up with the distinction of what was considered "sissy" (like dance, poetry, singing) and "manly" (football, wrestling, baseball) clearly delineated. And on the reverse end of things, that a man as artful and intelligent as Plato would carry with him a nickname taken from the world of combat sports, even after his days of competition were over, speaks volumes to the weight of value the Greeks placed on pursuits of both the body and the mind. Plato's teacher, Socrates was, after all, an accomplished wrestler, and not only in his youth.

Nicknames are funny things. Growing up I always wanted one, as it meant somebody cared enough to give it to me. Often, it's as simple as a physical characteristic (in the case of Plato's broad shoulders), but other times it's descriptive of one's abilities (such as the god Apollo's epithet "distant deadly archer"). The same holds true now. At my first gym, the coach had a nickname for everyone, to the point I hardly knew anyone's real name—they were only ever "Ironman," "Chuck Norris," "Panda." He gave me mine, "Clean Cut Jesus" (which as far as nicknames go, isn't as bad as some of his names for others— "Shamu" being a particularly embarrassing one) after only a day on the mats because (I can only assume) my short-trimmed beard and generic face reminded him of traditional images of Jesus.

In my second gym there were *nine* Joshes, so nicknames helped differentiate between the brown belt Josh who lived for talking shit (Hollywood), the big gangly blue belt Josh (Stickman), the white belt Josh who taught music (Little Drummer Boy), the purple belt Josh who happened to be fifth in the ranks (J-5), or myself, who made it easy on everybody by not shortening my name (Joshua).

Beyond making it easier to remember the people who came to the gym, it also serves a number of different purposes. First, it allows for a kind of rebranding, of claiming for oneself as a coach the person who's just started training (much in the way Plato's wrestling coach claimed him in his own renaming). Like the uniforms and crew-cuts of modern militaries, nicknaming in this sense strips a person of their individuality so they can be remade from the ground up; a new Jiu Jitsu creation, so to speak. Secondly, and perhaps most importantly, it has the potential to challenge the ego, especially if the nickname is embarrassing (or if, in the case of my own nickname, the coach is particularly fond of putting you in mounted crucifixes). Jiu Jitsu itself is a massive check on the ego, for reasons I'm sure everyone who's ever been stuck in a bottom position can understand, but when you're being shouted down as "Rat" or "Shamu" by your coach from the sidelines, the humiliation can take on a new level of significance.

On the other side, a nickname also has the power to positively solidify one's identity, either in its opposite (losing weight and learning how to fight might turn the moniker "Shamu" into something funny rather than demeaning), or in its actual nature (there's nothing demeaning about being nicknamed "Chuck Norris," but when you can actually kick ass like him, it makes it even more of a point of pride).

A nickname can simultaneously distinguish you from *and* solidify your place in the group. My buddies from the gym that I keep in touch with still call me "Jesus," and

"Chuck Norris" will always be "Chuck" to me, rather than "Jason", his real name. Nicknames serve as a means of bonding the group, of distinguishing members from their identities outside of the gym.

For figures of Greek mythology, who are unknowable outside of their stories, their heroic epithets (a fancy word for nicknames) give us a way of understanding essential aspects of their characters. These descriptions are persistent, not dependent on context. Thus the famous warrior Achilles is known both as "son of Peleus" and "swift-footed"—even in contexts where he is not running, because the epithet is permanent and portable for all occasions. Likewise, his rival and eventual victim Hector is "breaker of horses" and "shepherd of the people." The god Hephaestus is "the lame god" but he's also "the famous craftsman." Menelaus, king of the Spartans, is "red-haired" and "of the loud shout." Odysseus, who may have the most epithets of any figure in Greek mythology, is variously nicknamed "wise," "resourceful," "of many tricks," "sacker of cities," "great teller of tales," "hotheaded," and "man of pain"—so, knowing nothing of Odysseus, one might accurately guess at the kind of character he is (and his remarkable ability to disguise himself and his motives) based solely on his many nicknames.

In Mixed Martial Arts, nicknames are often fearsome ("The Axe Murderer," "The Iceman," "Rampage," "The Natural Born Killer"), which add to the mystique of the fighter, but they can also be quirky, and sometimes funny ("Uncle Creepy," "Violent Bob Ross," "Mighty Mouse," "Juicebox"). Nicknames create for fighter and fan alike a narrative not unlike those the Greeks would have been familiar with among their favorite heroes.

OUT OF THE CAVE

I talked about descending into the basement when entering my New York gym... in Plato's *Republic*, one of the more famous allegories Socrates develops for his listeners is that of the Cave. The allegory is traditionally understood as representing humanity's potential to progress from their inherent ignorance based on false assumptions (in the darkness of the Cave) into the light of reality and true knowledge (out in the bright Sun). For those who are unfamiliar with it, the gist is this: there are a group of people chained to a wall inside a Cave. They have been chained like this their entire lives. On the wall in front of them are shadowy figures being projected from behind them by other people holding those objects up to a fire so that their shadows pass in front of the eyes of the prisoners. The shadows are their only reality, and they believe the shadows to be true representations of actual objects. Socrates explains that a philosopher

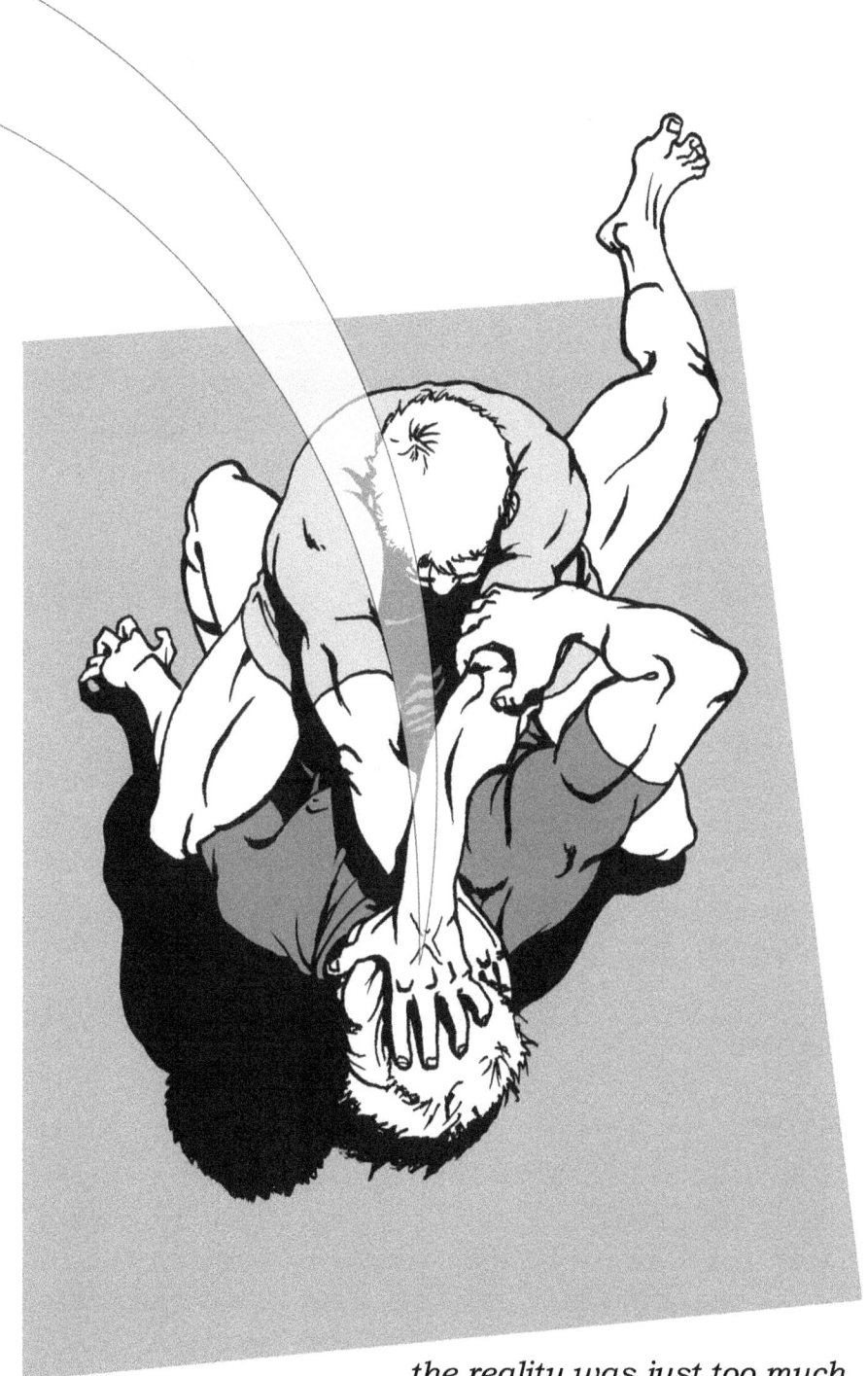

the reality was just too much

(literally, "lover of wisdom") is someone who, having freed themselves from their chains, realizes the illusory nature of the shadows they thought were real and proceeds by gradual steps out of the Cave up to the outside world, where they encounter the Sun for the first time and real objects instead of mere shadows. The intense brightness takes some getting used to, but elated by the discovery of the world of true knowledge, the philosopher attempts to cajole his former fellow prisoners into following him out of the Cave, but they are uninterested, preferring instead the shadows they've known their entire lives. But how does this nearly 2500-year-old story relate to our Mixed Martial Arts and Brazilian Jiu Jitsu journey? There's a lot to be unpacked here, so let's get started.

The journey from ignorance to enlightenment seems the best place to begin. I've explained previously my surprise at discovering in Brazilian Jiu Jitsu a radically different approach to self-defense, especially in relation to my previous experience as a boxer, but going even further back, I'd like to talk about my brief stint in Krav Maga, and then return to my initial impressions of grappling.

Before I started boxing, and long before I had any conception of which martial arts were most effective, like most untrained people fed a load of bull from media influences, I assumed Krav Maga would be the most effective means of self-defense. After all, at first glance it makes sense—strike at the most sensitive parts of a person and they're likely to leave you alone. So, having signed up for an introductory class I proceeded into the gym, which doubled as an MMA training facility. On the left of our class there were an odd group of people dressed in what looked like pajamas rolling around on the ground. I asked my instructor what their deal was, and he told me it was a Brazilian Jiu Jitsu class. I remember distinctly that it looked like the most boring thing I'd ever seen; that I'd never be caught dead groping around with other dudes on the ground. Next to the elbows and punches we were throwing in the Krav Maga class, it seemed incredibly silly. This was my time in the Cave, content with my understanding of the "shadows on the wall."

Flash forward several years, and I'm in the basement of my first gym, experiencing an entirely different introductory class. Since I've already gone into detail about that first experience, I just want to relate my felt impressions of being manhandled for the first time, and how they relate to Socrates' allegory. I remember distinctly the feelings of helplessness, the reality that if my instructor wanted to, he could hold me in place indefinitely and do whatever he pleased for as long as he pleased. Then my mind ranged to the wider world, thinking of how many blue, purple, brown, and black belts there were walking around, and I was overwhelmed by the implications of those everyday ninjas and what they were capable of. It was a stark awakening to reality akin to taking my first steps into the outside world, having lived the previous twenty-five years in veritable darkness. It's no exaggeration to say that nearly every day for the first several weeks I thought about quitting. The reality was just too much.

No doubt many of us have experienced the same sensation. Recently I was talking with a buddy of mine ("Chuck Norris" of the previous chapter on nicknames), sharing the feelings of being overwhelmed:

> Me: "I thought about quitting every day. I realized the scope of what I was getting into and it seemed like it was way too much to even try to learn."
>
> Chuck: "I still think about quitting for the same reasons. All the time."

But it's not just the reality of what elite tier Jiu Jitsu practitioners are capable of, but also the nature of Jiu Jitsu itself which serves as a consistent reminder to "Check yourself before you wreck yourself." Incredibly complex, with a seemingly never-ending series of moves and counter-moves, the sheer scope of Jiu Jitsu's catalog of techniques is daunting. It's like, having exited the Cave, one is not only confronted for the first time with the overwhelming light of the Sun, but one is then required to distinguish the new and uniquely perfect objects—tree and river and animal etc., here represented by mastery of the many possible techniques and positions available.

But there is still a further layer of analysis: that of one's own physical limitations. Recently at our gym we've had an influx of new people, mostly students from the local college. As a gym in a college town, we get a lot of young guys a little too overconfident in their capabilities. My policy when rolling with new guys is similar to that of Chewy's, from the popular *Chewjitsu* YouTube channel:

smash them fast and hard for the first few minutes of a round to let them know you know what you're doing, and that any previous ideas they had about their own ability to defend themselves are likely ineffectual. So, that's what I did. While still rolling with the quickly exhausted first guy, he muttered, "this is really emasculating." After finishing a round with the second guy, he slapped the mat in frustration, yelling expletives as he retreated to the sidelines. It was a night of rude awakenings. Having had no previous experience of grappling, these two guys immediately expected to be able to handle themselves against someone who had been practicing Jiu Jitsu for nearly seven years. Blinded by the light of the Sun and reality of life outside the Cave, their reactions were despair and anger, respectively. We'll see if they keep coming back.

But Jiu Jitsu does that, and not just to new guys. I'm constantly humbled by my lack of knowledge, my physical limitations, and my often-unimaginative technique chain. I look back on the unfortunate video evidence of my tournament victories and think "what a boring way to win," or "why didn't I do this or that differently?" But the more time one spends on the mat, the more one is able to adjust to the light of the Sun and the distinct objects of the real world. The mat *really is* the truth, I couldn't agree more. But how exactly do we go about experiencing that truth aside from a confrontation with our limitations? I believe the answer is also found in Socrates' allegory.

For anyone who's read Plato's *Republic* a consistent feature presents itself over and over again, often to the annoyance of the reader—that of *relentless* conversation and interrogation. Socrates questions everyone and everything, but not simply to be annoying (though I'm sure he relishes that too—he actually refers to himself as a "horsefly" pestering the city of Athens, stinging it, like some noble steed grown lazy, into taking action and improving its condition).[24] He engages in dialogue in order to come to a better understanding of the truth of the world—whether it's the nature of power, the role of artists in society, or what the ideal city-state might look like. His knowledge isn't based on sitting alone in the dark contemplating the world, but emerging into the light to talk with his fellows. And it's in this analogy that I think we come to the crux of how Brazilian Jiu Jitsu functions in our lives. After all, what is Jiu Jitsu but a kind of relentless physical dialogue? "I move, then you move, then I move, then you move, forever" is a popular quote I'm sure many of us have heard about the ideal roll. For those of us who manage to stick around long enough, enduring the consistent humiliation and ego-death, the mat is the ground of conversation on which we gradually acclimate ourselves to life outside the Cave, striving with our fellows to grab hold of truth and force it to submission.[25]

In one of Plato's dialogues, the *Theaetetus*, Socrates engages with the mathematics teacher (Theodorus) of the youth after whom the work is named, and the subject is how knowledge is to be acquired. Theodorus complains at one point that Socrates goes much further than the Spartan warning inscribed at the entrance to their gymnasia—*Strip down or Go Away*—because he doesn't even give his interlocutors the option of leaving and forces them "to wrestle with him in words." No, says Theodorus, Socrates is actually more like Sciron—a notorious bandit along the road to Athens who forced travelers to wash his feet and then booted them into the sea (until Theseus killed him in the same manner). Or he is like Antaeus (whose name means simply "Opponent"), who challenged everyone who came his way to a wrestling-match: he always won, as long as he remained in contact with his mother (the Earth), i.e., on the ground. Hercules, realizing that throwing or pinning would not work in this case, finally defeated him by hoisting him up in a bear-hug and squeezing him to death.

Socrates warmly approves of the comparisons Theodorus has used to describe his "disease" of asking questions and claims he is actually "stronger" or "more valiant" than Sciron or Antaeus since he's already run into a thousand versions of Theseus and Hercules who were "powerful in arguing" and who indeed "gave him a good beating" or "pounded" him. But he has no intention of stepping away from his "terrible passion" for such "argumentative workouts." The mention of Theseus and Hercules is especially clever here, since both heroes grappled with all kinds of challenging opponents and Theseus is credited with inventing wrestling, or adding to its list of techniques, in his bout with Cerycon—another notorious challenger like Antaeus, who forced travelers to enter his palaestra.[26] Another tradition suggests he created the style of fighting we see in the pankration, using all available means to eliminate his opponents. (See PLATE 5).

It's funny how elements of the competitive *agon* bleed into one another (sometimes literally). When I was getting my Masters in NYC, our classes were three hours long and always in the evenings. So, after long days of work at any one of my three jobs, I'd make the trek an hour or so from Brooklyn to the Upper East Side for class. Now don't get me wrong, grad school in the city was a blast: the classes were invigorating and the professors some of the best I've ever had—but regardless of how good the class was, I'd step outside afterwards feeling (at least mentally) as if I'd endured a competitive open mat or handful of tournament matches. Academic rigors, social interactions with my cohort, and meetings with professors were intellectually comparable to any of the innumerable physical rigors I've endured as an athlete.

And many times, after a poetry workshop or literature course, I'd take the train across town to Radical MMA and catch the last thirty-to-forty-five minutes of a Jiu Jitsu class, get some good rolls in, and head home for the evening (or stick around to clean the gym). Unfortunately for my teammates, if it was a particularly patience-testing evening at Hunter, I'd stroll into the gym ready for a fight, eager to take out my academic frustrations on the mat. Thankfully, as a small-ish, still fresh white belt, how much damage could I really do?

Flash forward to this morning: I'm home for Christmas break and decide to head over to the local Checkmat gym where I've made some friends and like to roll whenever I'm in town. They have a morning MMA class, so when I get there I pull on my gloves and get to work running drills and practicing my footwork. Later in the class comes the inevitable beatdown sparring sessions, with some teammates unable to restrain themselves. As strange as it may sound, I relish the opportunity to test my chin and improve my striking skills occasionally, so I stand and bang with Johnny One-Speed (Q: why do they call him Johnny One-Speed? A: because he only has one speed). Being the thoroughly amateur striker that I am, I take a beating, getting my bell rung more than once or twice.

At the end of practice, I retrieve my phone and see I've got some messages from none other than the co-author of this book, my good chum David. He always wants updates from my adventures in the *agon*, so I fill him in on how the morning is progressing, concussions and all. We begin our usual back and forth of witticisms and gibes (or jabs) over text until he makes the astute observation that, "Funny how physical striking leads seamlessly to verbal striking, thus proving the theory of the *agon*." And boom like a light bulb (or like the stars I was seeing after a few of Johnny's straight right hands), the synapses flashed and connections were made: for those of us with a competitive drive, one *agon* leads to another, in succession, endlessly. While we're not privy to the daily routine of Socrates and his cohort, one can imagine a routine through "realms of antagonism" similar to what I've just described—perhaps a workout in the morning, maybe with some light sparring in boxing or wrestling, and in the afternoon a series of verbal exchanges which would eventually comprise the dialogues Plato has preserved for us.

Every collaboration is an *agon*, a struggle towards a common goal by different routes. Whether it's a collaboration towards greater wisdom like the Socratic dialogues of the *Republic*, or towards the conquest of an enemy combatant like the famously antagonistic Greek heroes of the *Iliad*, or even towards the sharpening of one's athletic skills in a combat sports gym, every collaboration necessarily involves the concord and clashing of disparate (and often volatile) personalities.

In Book 1 of the *Republic*, Socrates gathers to himself a small cohort of amateur philosophers, sophists, and bystanders to discuss the definition of justice. He questions each individually, and receives wildly different answers: justice is "giving what is owed," "rewarding friends and punishing enemies," and "the will of the strong." His relentless questioning reveals the flaws in each definition. Socrates however, being the "coach" among this crowd, takes the disparate answers and unites them later into his own vision for the just city, his own ideal republic.

The *Iliad* begins with a fight in the midst of a massive collaborative effort: the Greeks' siege of the city of Troy. In Book 1, Achilles is enraged over a seeming wrong done to him by king Agamemnon, and threatens violence. Only the intervention of cooler heads (the elder Nestor) keeps the dispute from erupting into bloodshed. But Achilles storms out nonetheless, refusing to take further part in the war. The entirety of the epic is a series of failed attempts at sacking Troy until the ultimate return of Achilles to the army and his killing of Hector, whereupon the project is destined to be brought to completion and the city ultimately destroyed.

And of course, the work we put in at the gym, while it may seem highly individualized, is in fact collaborative. No blackbelt has ever achieved their rank on their own (even *Gracie Online* requires the occasional visit to an actual gym), and no Jiu Jitsu gym exists in a vacuum. Our entire enterprise of personal development is ironically dependent on our coaches and training partners. Who hasn't learned the unfortunate lesson to roll cautiously with the big uncoordinated white belt? (If you haven't yet, you will eventually). Who hasn't encountered at a tournament an opponent far beyond their own skill levels? And seemingly unrelated to practicing Jiu Jitsu, who hasn't grown close with the cohort of killers at their gyms, going out for beers or food occasionally, busting balls and talking about relationships, the latest conspiracy theories, psychology, politics, or any number of unrelated topics with the same enthusiasm as they talk about Jiu Jitsu? The agonistic space is equally the collaborative.

And in my own teaching career, since I usually make my extracurricular activities known to my students in some form or another (most often in the icebreaker game: "My name is Mr. Kulseth and I train combat sports"), some of them have sought me out for advice on how or where to get started. Of course, I recommend my own gym in town, and as it happens, some of them have actually joined so I can claim, along with Socrates, to have trained (or abused) the minds and bodies of my students. Thus, we swing from one *agon* to another.

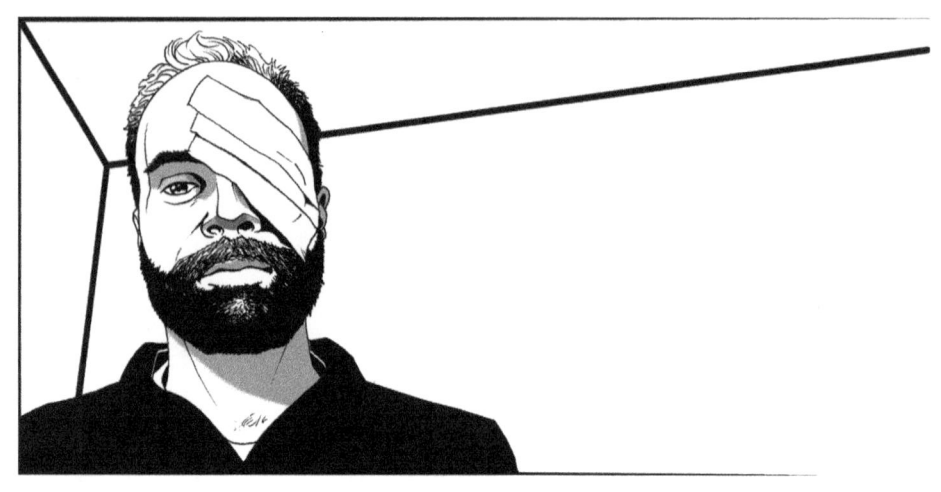

A POKE IN THE EYE

I've worn glasses since middle school, and over the years my vision has gotten progressively worse to the point that without them it's all blur and smudge. Having corrective lenses presented a new set of problems when I started doing combat sports. During boxing I'd go without my glasses when working the bags or pads, and on sparring days I'd wear contacts, but after a few well-placed jabs a lens might pop out, leaving me half-blinded for the rest of the round, depth-perception and timing all out of whack so it was really only a matter of minimizing the damage taken rather than presenting an actual threat. During my blessedly short-lived boxing career (to this day, my record stands at an impressive 0-1), I learned that in the rules of amateur competition no sort of corrective lens was permitted. In my training camp, I sparred how I knew I'd have to fight, and discovered a strange sensation: when my sparring partners

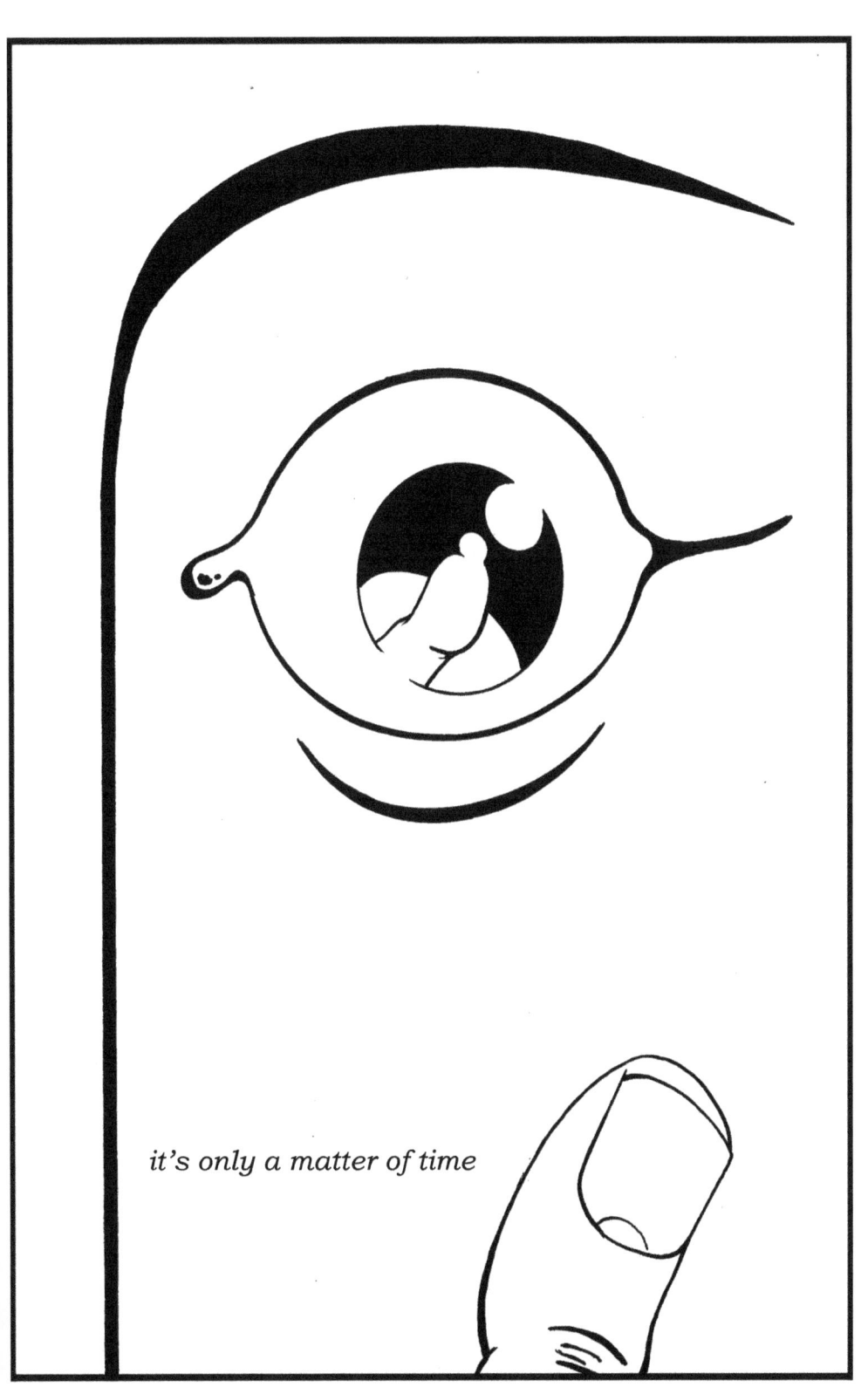

were blurred so I could only make out the most basic movements, it actually made engaging in the fight easier. It made me less cautious, so I was actually more willing to trade shots, less skittish or susceptible to feints. Having compromised vision opened up to me a new freedom, and while it ultimately didn't help me much in the tournament, the sensation has stayed with me through boxing and into my time as a grappler.

In my experience, getting eye-poked is a fairly common occurrence in grappling sports, more so than one might initially expect (much in the same way I once thought I'd get fewer concussions in Jiu Jitsu than I did in boxing, which sadly proved untrue). With limbs splayed and flailing in all directions, it's only a matter of time before something finds its way into an eyeball. I've had my fair share, and have had to fish the occasional contact lens from off the mat, or worse, from somewhere under my eyelid. After I got PRK corrective surgery, my fears were amplified, not wanting in some way to ruin the newly-gained 20/20 vision. But, inevitably, a finger found its way, most often in my botched shots—a double-leg turning quickly into a half-blind scramble for bottom quarter-guard.

But vision is a funny thing, especially in Jiu Jitsu (in wrestling of course it helps to be able to actually see the opponent you're shooting on). Much like my experience in boxing, I found my impeded vision to be a kind of advantage in my growth as a fighter. While I was recovering, I found it was less painful, once on the ground, to close both of my eyes than to try to keep only one open. While limiting, it was surprisingly helpful in a number of ways: it improved the fluidity of my movement, as I was less concerned over my opponents' various twitches or spasms, or even of their facial expressions, whether pained or determined. It also improved my technique, as I didn't have the luxury of sight to assure myself of a position, and had to feel my way into a pin or submission. Lastly, I was more relaxed, and even my breathing became steadier. Rather than fear, closing my eyes seemed to have the opposite effect. I remember as a fresh blue belt being somewhat taken aback when I was repeatedly submitted by a blind purple belt I'd encountered at a new gym, but it began to make more sense as I encountered my own body (and that of my opponent) with exclusively tactile perception. Earlier I mentioned my "poker face" and how emotions are not written all over the face, either in Classical Greek sculpture or in the midst of combat. Not looking directly at one's opponent is, in fact, the norm.

Sight, whether literal or metaphorical, figures heavily in Greek storytelling. From Prometheus, whose name means "foresight," to Polyphemus, the great Cyclops whose single eye was blinded by Odysseus, to Tiresias, the blind prophet who foretold the downfall (and self-blinding) of Oedipus, famous for his anger and questionable choice in women, to the hundred-eyed monster Argus *Panoptes* (meaning, "all-seeing"), whose eyes were said to have been preserved by the goddess Hera in the tail of a peacock after his death, Greek mythology had no shortage of heroes and villains with various sight issues.

The Titan Prometheus is most commonly known for stealing fire from the gods in order to give it to humankind. He also knew the secret of Zeus' future downfall at the hands of a son "greater than himself" he would produce with a goddess. As a consequence, he was nailed to a remote rock and cursed by Zeus to have his immortal liver eaten by an eagle every day for all time. According to the myth, he was eventually released after agreeing to share with Zeus the name of the goddess in question—Thetis, who would go on to have a son with Peleus instead, namely, Achilles. Zeus was forced to compromise in some way. Thanks to his "foresight," Prometheus had outfoxed the king of the gods, securing his own release, as well as the protection and prosperity of humanity through his various gifts.[27]

Less commonly known is Prometheus' role, according to our friend Philostratus, in the creation of the sport of wrestling. A strategic thinker who outmaneuvered even the most powerful Olympian god in a contest of wits and will, it's no surprise to discover that according to legend, he invented a sport requiring intelligence, will power, and strategy, as opposed to brute strength alone. When Prometheus is banished to the rock, he is pinned to it by his arms, chest, torso, legs and feet; in other words, he is completely immobilized and thus denied all capacity to act in the physical realm. Zeus may be *pankrates*, all-powerful (just like the *pankration*), yet Prometheus' insight into the future, and his refusal to give into physical torment and humiliation, enable him to force Zeus into negotiation and to set him free. Philostratus' account of the invention of wrestling makes interesting reading: he starts from the proposition that *gymnastike* (physical training) is "inborn" and develops along with humankind. Prometheus begins by training himself before he creates humans whom he molds from earth (the very "mud" or "dust" on which wrestlers fought); then, they say, Hermes is the first to train others how to wrestle and is said to have created the first palaestra.[28] Hermes is frequently associated with gymnasiums and athletic contests, and is known as the "Trickster" among the Olympian gods, inheriting Prometheus' role.

Jiu Jitsu, a close relative of wrestling, and with a similar focus on immobilization and escape that we also find in the pankration, has a number of descriptive metaphors attached to it. More often than not, these analogies contain a common thread which distinguishes them: intelligence, and a capacity for strategic thinking amid multiple threats. BJJ requires clever escapes from impossible holds and applying pressure by "tricky" means. For the Greeks, who valued the life of the mind over mere physicality, the figure of the trickster, or the cunning strategist, was a particular favorite. So, while Zeus the overlord of Olympus and patriarch of the gods was honored among mortals, Prometheus was the one who was imitated and admired as the benefactor of humankind.

Trickery and deception were highly regarded in Greek culture, and it was those wiliest of thinkers who are most fondly remembered—like Odysseus, who brainstormed the ultimate deception, the Wooden Horse which helped the Greeks sack Troy. He could assess a situation—an impasse, a trap, a lethal "hold"—and use his wits to devise a way out. On his journey home after the Trojan War, he blinds the giant Polyphemus with a (red-hot) "poke in the eye" and thus he and his men escape from the Cyclops' cave where they had been imprisoned. He may be taking a leaf out of Hercules' playbook: a vase-painting shows him grabbing the beard of Antaeus and gouging his eyes in their wresting-match. Interestingly, deliberately poking or gouging the eye seems to have been generally viewed in Greece as breaking the rules, as we sometimes (but not always) see a trainer or referee intervening to stop it. (See PLATE 6). In Sparta, however, such techniques, along with biting, may have been allowed in their city gymnasiums.[29]

When leglocks first exploded on to the Jiu Jitsu scene (exploded, along with a lot of knees), the community was divided over their legitimacy—were they merely a gimmick for people who couldn't pass guard, or were they viable techniques? Regardless of how we initially felt, their efficacy was undeniable, as a new generation of leglockers systematically dismantled the old guard of smash passers. Jiu Jitsu is ever-evolving, patterned in terms of thesis and antithesis: a technique is presented, and its counter is quickly discovered, on and on, seemingly forever. The nature of Jiu Jitsu is subversive, as Helio Gracie's first techniques were developed for the smaller, less naturally gifted student. It will always be the tricksters, the ones with foresight and determination, who will move the sport forward.

One is reminded of Greek fighters whose unusual techniques are recorded: Sostratus of Sicyon, nicknamed "Fingers" or "Fingerman," won several victories in the pankration by bending back the fingers of his opponent, thereby controlling his movement and forcing him to submit.[30] Leontiscus ("little lion') used the same technique to similar effect, winning the wrestling at Olympia. We also hear of a pankratiast from Cilicia, nicknamed "Jumping-Weight" (because he was much smaller than his opponents, though well-shaped and quite strong) who asked an oracle how he could defeat them and was told "by getting trampled": this meant "not letting go of the foot" because if you "wrestle with the heel" you must constantly "get trampled and be under your opponent." Perhaps the original heel-hooker?[31] In fact, as we will elaborate shortly below, Brazilian Jiu Jitsu is *the trickster sport* and Odysseus its hero. But let's think a little more about the hero and his journey first.

DEATH AND REBIRTH

Waking up after getting choked out is a trip. For those who've never experienced it (don't worry, it'll happen eventually), it's like coming out of a dream, and it often takes a few seconds of adjustment in order to make it all the way back to reality—"What happened," "Did I win?"—in cage fights you might see someone regain consciousness only to start fighting again, either with his opponent or the ref, not realizing until later exactly what happened. It's like being in a different world altogether.

Unsurprisingly, the language of strangling, suffocation and drowning is very common in the world of Brazilian Jiu Jitsu. Phrases like "drowning on dry land" and "entering the shark tank" are heard in every gym.[32] Greek wrestlers and pankratiasts used all kinds of headlocks and neck holds and had their own vocabulary of suffocation and strangling: The Greek comic writer Lucian imagines a visitor from Persia, Anacharsis, looking with amazement upon young Athenians wrestling at the gymnasium of the Lyceum (where Plato and Aristotle hung out): they are locked together, tripping or strangling or twisting one another and rolling around in the mud like pigs. They push against each other and butt their heads together like rams. One picks up another by the legs and throws him to the ground then falls down upon him and doesn't let him get up, pushing him down into the mud. He wraps his legs around his opponent's waist, places his forearm under his throat, strangling him, as the other taps his shoulder, begging, so he doesn't get suffocated completely. Others, standing up, strike and kick each other, one gets hit on the jaw and his mouth is full of blood and sand, but the official does not break up the fight, in fact he praises the one who landed the blow.[33]

In Greek mythology, the hero's journey often includes a trip to the Underworld. Whether it's Hercules' final labor of bagging the great three-headed hell-dog Cerberus, or Theseus' attempt to rescue the kidnapped Persephone, or even Odysseus just heading down for a little chat with the dead prophet Tiresias and warrior Achilles, a critical aspect of growth for the hero is his descent to the dark Land of the Dead. But the descent is only half the journey, after all. No heroes would be worth their salt if they couldn't manage to get back out again, returning to the upper world of light and life with new knowledge, new friends, or even a new pet hell-dog.

Likewise on the mats (and not only for those who are either too green or too stubborn to tap and wind up taking an involuntary nap), death and rebirth, descent and ascent, are just part of the experience in Jiu Jitsu gyms. After all, what does it mean to tap to a submission? As I mentioned earlier, is it not the acknowledgement that my partner has "killed" me? That I've lost, and must begin again? And with that new beginning hopefully comes new knowledge; a new perspective on both the literal techniques (what can I do better next time to prevent my opponent from killing me), as well as oneself and one's place on the mats. One discovers the reality of mortality over and over again, day after day, year after year, for however long you practice the sport, and that new knowledge inevitably (hopefully) shapes that person into a better version of themselves for having faced and overcome their natural limitations.

Even if the journey is a failure (tapping is also an admittance of failure)—Theseus' rescue attempt failed, and he in turn had to be rescued by Hercules; Orpheus' attempt to bring his dead wife Eurydice back to the world of the living equally failed—and even if the Underworld has more sorrow than glory to offer, nonetheless *the attempt itself* is commemorated as a feat of great strength. In words taken from Vergil's *Aeneid*: "Easy is the way down to Hell, for the door to the Underworld is open day and night, but to retrace your steps, to come back to the breezes above, that's a task, that's the hard work." As for Orpheus, he becomes the embodiment of the power of poetry, of art: his enchanting song after all persuaded Hades to allow him to take his wife back up with him and, although he failed (he broke the taboo Hades had trickily imposed against looking back behind him on the way up and Eurydice was lost forever), the myth is the most powerful depiction we have of the triumph of art over death.

One ancient fighter, the pankratiast Arrichion, is well known and much celebrated in MMA circles. He had won the crown at Olympia in 572 and 568 BC and in 564 returned to defend his title in a sensational *agon*. The Greek writer Pausanias describes how in the last round of the competition Arrichion's opponent trapped him between his legs and squeezed his neck until he suffocated—but not before Arrichion broke the toe of his opponent who "tapped" at the same moment. The Olympic judges placed the victor's crown on Arrichion's lifeless body. Philostratus gives us a similar account derived from a painting, with the opponent trapping his legs and choking him, with a foot inside each knee until, taking advantage of some loosening in the leg scissors, Arrichion kicked out with his right foot, locked the opponent's foot inside his own knee and shifting his weight leftwards ripped the ankle out of its socket. Neither version has proved entirely convincing to modern analysts, and speculation about exactly what happened continues, but the core of the story is the same: that Arrichion managed to cause excruciating, submission-generating pain by hooking the foot of his opponent, even as the life was choked out of him. Death *and* Victory simultaneously. Philostratus in his other work, *Gymnastike*, adds that Arrichion's trainer bore some responsibility for the outcome by shouting out "what a noble funeral shroud this would be for you—not to be submitted at Olympia!" right at the moment when Arrichion was about to give up. And indeed Arrichion was memorialized with a statue in his hometown, no doubt the hero of the local palaestra and gymnasium, and he has been remembered to this day.[34]

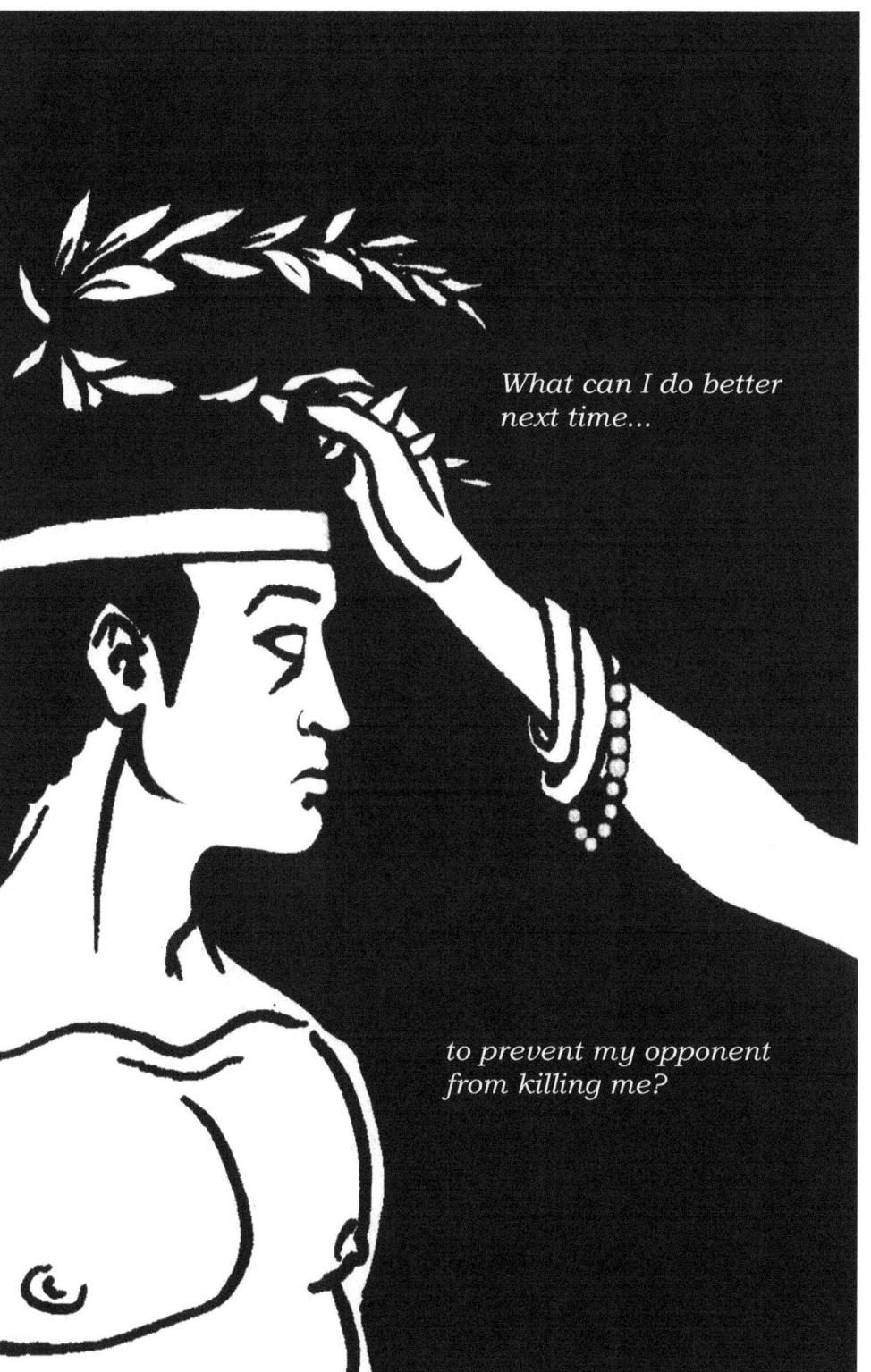

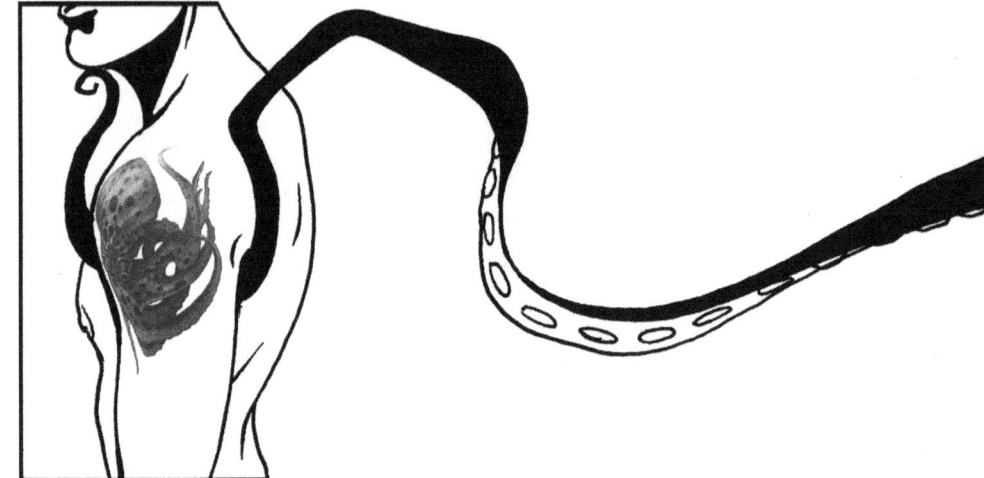

INK

Choosing your first Jiu Jitsu themed tattoo is a big deal. You have to think:
1. Do I enjoy this sport enough to put a permanent advertisement on my body?
2. Do I plan to keep training? It would be a shame to have to explain to people the meaning of a Jiu Jitsu tattoo only to have to then admit that you stopped training years ago.
3. Will it make me look like an enormous tool, on par with the people who wear Tap-Out or American Fighter gear?
4. And most importantly, what artwork might be best representative of who I am as a grappler?

Often associated with the question are the corresponding animal images: gorilla, anaconda, octopus, honey badger (the latter being the particular favorite of my smaller training partners). What best describes my grappling "method"—do I blitz opponents like a gorilla;

do I slowly but consistently constrict and solidify position like an anaconda; or do I set traps, using feints to bait my opponents into inescapable submissions like an octopus?

More often than not, body type and levels of endurance are the determining factors (for instance, while there are exceptions, most of my training partners weighing over 200lbs generally fit into the gorilla category), but preferred submissions, injuries, or even your fellow training partners can equally affect the type of Jiu Jitsu game you develop.

I was always on the smaller side, averaging around 155lbs. Most of my training partners have not only been larger than me, but *much* larger, often in excess of 190lbs. My style developed accordingly: kimuras and other joint locks were generally out of the question, as I'd either get stacked out of an armbar or flexed out of a kimura. Guillotines were tough because my scrawny arms couldn't hang on long enough around the thick necks of my opponents. Leg-locks were great, but I didn't start learning those until two years after I'd started training. So, for me, triangles and rear-naked chokes were my go-to—if I could get to my guard or to my opponent's back, I worked hard to stay there, becoming ever more threatening as I improved. I also learned quickly that with training partners like mine, if I got into a good position, I had to learn how to keep it or risk getting crushed for the rest of the round.

So, after a year and a half of training, with my first tournament recently under my belt (a desperate exhibition which nevertheless earned me a silver medal win via triangle choke), I'd decided on a small symbol, placed on my ribs (regretfully as I would later find out, sweating and writhing, "tough" fighter that I was, under the tattoo needle)—it was a silhouette I'd found on the internet of a rear-naked choke. It was appropriate enough for who I thought I was at the time, a no-frills kind of white belt who preferred the stable, unflashy win to the cartwheels, gogoplatas, and flying armbars of some of my teammates. With that, I was roped in for the long run, determined to be a competitor, with the sick new ink to prove it. Watch out, Monster-guzzling Kyles of the world, this was one pip-squeak you didn't want to cross.

Philostratus talks of certain athletes who are "big in small": smaller in size, but "with well-structured bodies which look large" and whose skills can be observed in wrestling because they are flexible (*eustrophos*, easily turning, nimble), versatile (*polutropos*, of many tricks—like Odysseus), vigorous (*sphodros*), light (*kouphos*), quick (*tachys*), and uniform (*homotonos*, having the same force, tone throughout the body).[35] They are able to escape from many impossible situations, hard to wrestle out of, by "supporting themselves on their heads as if on their feet"—this sounds like Philostratus' description of a bridge and hip escape. He cites Maron of Cilicia as an example (who may be our previously mentioned "Jumping-Weight" celebrity), probably for his nimble movement around larger, bulkier and stronger opponents.

In a similar vein, Pindar in his *Isthmian Ode 4* writes in praise of Melissos of Thebes, a victorious pankratiast:

he has the "boldness of loud-roaring lions in his spirit" during the struggle of the *agon*, but has the *metis* (skill, cunning) of a fox when he rolls on his back defending himself against the "swooping eagle," adding that you have to do everything you can "to diminish" the opponent."[36] Pindar goes on to explain why: Melissos was not blessed with the body of an Orion (son of Poseidon and the mighty hunter of Greek myth). But, while you might "scorn" his slight appearance, he was "heavy in his strength" if you fell into combat with him. To make the point, the poet invites a comparison with Hercules, "short in stature but unbending in his spirit," who went to wrestle Antaeus and killed him.[37] It is the versatility of the "large in small" combined with a fierce inner determination which carries them to victory—a process of gradually and irreversibly "diminishing" the opponent, of "dimming his lights." Not everyone who trained (or discussed philosophy) in the so-called "Gymnasium of the Giants" in Athens, with its massive sculptures of kneeling Giants, would have been huge in stature, but the imagery is obviously aspirational, as even those who were "small" could become formidable well beyond their size.

Having a bit of a Napoleon complex, it was always a point of pride to be told I had "the pressure of a much larger dude," and as my Jiu Jitsu game developed, I solidified more and more into the type of grappler who preferred the slow and steady race, working my way to the eventual constriction. I'd smash pass past half guard into side-control, holding out against the desperate bucking spasms of big guys, cross-facing until I felt confident enough in my control to slide a knee across their belly into full mount. From there, it was a matter of weathering the storm until the back-take presented itself. By the time I'd taken the back, I found the submission fairly quickly. So, as I collected displaced ribs, dislocated fingers, and knee injuries, I thought it was high time for the next installment of visual signification in the form of a more complex tattoo.

Given the type of grappler I'd developed into, a particularly tireless cuddler, I was leaning most towards an *octopus* for my personal emblem. Being one of the more common visual metaphors for the sport, the octopus had found its way permanently onto many-a-grappler's skin, most famously on the ribs of Craig Jones (under which is written "Arte Suave"—the ironic, Gentle Art), which I noticed for the first time watching his ADCC debut.

And so, after some six hours, an octopus, rendered in black and white, found its way onto my left shoulder, a single tentacle visible below the sleeve-line. As happens, I've gotten compliments from training partners who appreciate its design and concept, but most satisfyingly, many have commented that it's a fitting choice, considering the squeeze I most frequently put on them.

Animal imagery in Greek culture was as common, perhaps even more so than it is in our own, and everywhere in their iconography you're likely to find men and gods engaged in combat with half-animals (like the Minotaur or Centaurs), or like Hercules, with lions and giant serpents. Images of the owl, fish, bull, scorpion, and others adorned the shields of soldiers in Greek city-states. In Homer's epic poems the *Iliad* and the *Odyssey*, heroic epithets (those formal titles given to different gods or distinguished mortals) often had animal associations: "ox-eyed," "lion-hearted," "breaker of horses," "loud-roaring" and the like. As long as humanity has striven in contests, whether in sport, in war, or even in the arts, there have been accompanying descriptive analogies, more often than not associated with animals. Octopus imagery is very common on Greek pottery, especially from the Minoan era, often with the tentacles spreading all over the vase in wildly energetic fashion.

The ancient writer of a poem about fish and sea creatures, Oppian, describes how they are all bitter foes to each other and distinguishes between those that are powerful through great strength or weaponry (like stings or teeth) and others who rely upon "the weapon of the mind" and "crafty strategy of many devices" to destroy those bigger and stronger than themselves. Among these latter he singles out the octopus for praise for its ability to disguise itself and to deceive and mislead other fish, enabling it to avoid destruction. The octopus is locked in continual mutual battle with the sea-eel (*muraena*): the "raging" eel rushes forward with jaws full of sharp teeth ready to bite, while the octopus uses its tentacles to entwine its opponent. Oppian compares them to two skilled wrestlers locked in a long and sweaty struggle, using all their various skills and tricks as their hands flail around their bodies.[38]

The humanized version of the octopus is the shape-shifting "Old Man of the Sea" Proteus, with whom Menelaus grapples in Book 4 of the *Odyssey*. Proteus is immortal and possesses prophetic skills (rather like Prometheus), but can only be forced to disclose information by being pinned down and immobilized. He keeps changing shape—by turns a lion, serpent, leopard, pig, water, and a tree—but Menelaus clings on until Proteus divulges his secrets. The various forms he takes probably signify different kinds of grappling challenges or combat opponents. You can see how some grappling opponents might be like a lion, or a pig, or even water or a tree. We still use the term "protean" today to signify something which is continually changing or never in a settled state, and the notion of the slippery antagonist, hard to pin down or submit, finds an echo in the words of our verbal grappler Socrates to one of his interlocutors:[39] "You are a trickster, you have as many shapes as Proteus, twisting and turning in all directions, until you finally escape from me."

THE GOOD, THE BAD, AND THE STRANGER

Among the innumerable distractions available to a Ph.D. candidate looking to escape from work for a couple of hours, there are few as strangely useful in their distractions as the suggested videos section of YouTube. Like the adult version of *Schoolhouse Rock*, I often stumble across educational series masked in entertaining descriptions or eye-catching thumbnails. Recently I went down a rabbit hole of animal videos, both cute and horrifying (whether a mother hippo mauling a pride of lions or a Great Dane cowering before a kitten). In the previous chapter we talked about the kinds of animals a combat sports athlete might be likely to identify with—octopus, shark, gorilla etc.—but one which has been a particular personal favorite is the indomitable Honey Badger. If you haven't seen it already, stop reading immediately and search YouTube for the video "Fearless Honey Badger Takes on 6 Lions." You won't be disappointed. The title describes it perfectly: a single Honey Badger wanders into a pride of lions and proceeds to hiss and spit and claw and bite its way to a stalemate with a pack of bewildered apex predators. Badly mauled, but alive nonetheless, the Honey Badger scores what I would consider to be at least a moral victory, as it's allowed to retreat back into the bushes. There is, unsurprisingly, a *Honey Badger* gym in Las Vegas.

The comparison isn't a new one, and likely the image of the scrappy and persistent "little guy" at the gym has made its rounds in the gossip mill, fostering comparisons to their spirited counterpart wandering fearlessly through the African savanna. It's an image I've frequently identified with, but never more so than when I haplessly stumbled into my own lion's den in the form of a gym called The Vault, located just outside Philadelphia.

Let me paint a picture for you. Having taken a couple weeks off from training to eat and drink my way through Northern Italy, but still feeling the residual ego boost of a bronze medal at the IBJJF Nogi Masters Worlds competition as a purple belt, I decided to visit a local gym during a long layover in Philly while on my way back home. In spite of the six months which had elapsed since my entirely average performance at Worlds, and having let myself lapse out of shape (I suppose round is still a shape), I still believed I was relatively hot shit, able at least to put up enough of a fight to earn the respect of anybody I rolled against. Like the intrepid Honey Badger, brave but vastly overestimating its abilities, I walked into the lion's den with blind confidence, and by the end of the night I was alive, but had been badly mauled for my arrogance.

My point is that there's a skill in visiting a new gym, especially as a higher belt. It requires tact and deference, a smile and positive attitude. All of these traits, whether natural or assumed for the occasion, reduce the chance of injury at the hands of either the coach or the assigned "mat enforcer."

I've come to understand that it's an entirely reasonable practice for the coach of a gym to protect themselves and their gym by putting the visitor "in their place" so to speak by partnering them against the best they've got. It's a defense of both their most vulnerable members (typically white belts who don't know any better), as well as an assertion of the skill level of their higher belts. It's common practice, and it makes sense. And while I possess the aforementioned necessary qualities, and only rarely allow whatever levels of arrogance which may be inherent in me at the moment to leak out onto the mats, I learned that night there is another quality necessary for survival: the humility to admit when you're woefully outmatched, and to tap out early.

I've grown substantially less stubborn in my old age, so tapping early has gradually become easier and easier, when consideration of how awful I know I will feel the next morning takes a back seat to "proving myself," whatever that means—though of course I still have my Honey Badger moments. Needless to say, had I known how badly my mauling would have affected my basic motor skills for the next week, there would have been a lot more concessions on my part during my Philly excursion, though perhaps I wouldn't have this nifty *National Geographic* analogy so readily available.

Leo Tolstoy wrote that there are only two kinds of stories: a man goes on a journey, or a stranger comes to town. I want to talk about the stranger. I've shared my own anecdote, and perhaps it's unsurprising that ancient Greek mythology is full of its own stories of strangers coming to town, never without substantial consequences (positive and negative) for both hero and city.

On his journey home from the ten-year Trojan war, our supreme trickster Odysseus is put through the ringer by the gods, being forced into a number of ports, both friendly and hostile, over the course of an additional ten years. In Book 6 of the *Odyssey*, Odysseus eventually washes ashore in the land of the Phaeacians (modern Corfu, in northwestern Greece) where, disguised by the goddess Athena, he arrives at the court of king Alcinous. With his true identity still hidden from the king and his people, although his witty and sophisticated speech suggests that he is no ordinary visitor, Odysseus is invited the next day to participate in a series of athletic contests—boxing, wrestling, discus-throwing etc. Still overcome by the hardships of his long journey and the loss of his comrades, he refuses the invitation. At that point, some of the younger competitors begin to deride the old hero, claiming he no longer has what it takes to keep up with the young men in their games, whereupon Odysseus is filled with rage and accepts the challenge, successfully out-throwing everyone in the discus. Furious still, he gets in the face of the young athlete and tells him he'll beat him in anything else he wants to compete in for that matter. Later, when the poet Demodocus sings about the exploits of the heroes at Troy, Odysseus starts weeping and his identity is finally revealed to all.

At the conclusion of the epic, in yet another instance of concealed identity, when he finally returns to Ithaca after two decades away, Odysseus disguises himself as an old beggar—the best means of assessing the loyalty (or otherwise) of the family and servants he left behind. While in disguise in Book 18, he is ridiculed by the suitors at the palace and insulted by Irus, a brash beggar of long-standing who thinks that Odysseus is muscling-in on his patch. Antinous, the leader of the suitors, thinks a boxing match between the two would be fun to watch and thus Odysseus finds himself in a random challenge. When he takes off his rags revealing a surprisingly muscular physique (thighs, shoulders, chest and arms), Irus changes his mind and backs off, but the suitors shove him towards Odysseus. He considers killing Irus but, in order to avoid arousing suspicion, merely lands a single bone-crushing punch below the ear and hauls him outside into the courtyard. Odysseus duly receives some bread as a reward.[40] In this preliminary *agon* before the "big reveal," the physical signs on Odysseus' body (including the famous scar on his thigh) are there to be read by the suitors but of course they fail to do so.

The bloody finale of the *Odyssey* is well known, but here it is in brief: derided by the arrogant young suitors, it is in a contest where his prowess is once again displayed, when the free-loading suitors are challenged by Queen Penelope to string the bow of her long-lost husband (it's rumored only he can string and shoot it) and fire an arrow between a number of hollow axe-heads. Predictably unable to do so, the suitors slink back dejected as Odysseus, still disguised, strings the bow and fires the arrow perfectly. He then throws off his rags and reveals himself like a god of war, imposing in his strength and size (to the shock and horror of the young men). He proceeds to slaughter the gaggle of suitors in a massacre reminiscent of his time spent on the Trojan battlefields and reclaims his kingdom.

Consistent throughout is the theme of disguise and revelation, always in a trial of strength, and after a long series of dialogues. The seemingly irrelevant old man or beggar, without any physical indication of skill, miraculously takes center stage and bests his opponents, even those far younger than himself. These moments in the story correlate with moments in my own life—what I like to call "Oh, Shit!" moments—specifically in the gym, when I underestimated my opponents and promptly paid for it with an ass whooping. This admittedly happens less and less as I've learned not to judge a book by its cover, but in the past it happened frequently, with predictable results.

The *Odyssey* offers two instances in a single work of a stranger coming to town where the consequences are universally positive for the stranger and detrimental to those who have crossed him. This isn't always the case, either in real life or in Greek mythology. Let's look at another example.

In the Greek playwright Aeschylus' *Seven Against Thebes*, there are, predictably, seven heroes who lead an army against the ancient city of Thebes (which conveniently for the story also has seven gates manned by seven defending heroes) in order to restore Polynices, son of Oedipus, to the throne. The endeavor fails miserably, and the attacking heroes are repulsed by their respective foils at the gates, either dying spectacularly (like Capaneus, struck by Zeus' lightning bolt while mounting the walls), or being forced to retreat. The seven attackers are characterized by their arrogance and presumption that the city will be easily taken by such a mighty host, and their subsequent defeat presents a run-of-the-mill moral lesson to the reader about the consequences of overweening pride.

Sometimes you're the hammer, and sometimes you're the nail, is a popular enough aphorism in the Jiu Jitsu community, but it seems particularly apt in the case of strangers, who often take center stage in the unfolding drama of our gyms, as all eyes are on the newcomer, watching and waiting to see whether they turn out to be an Odysseus, taking on all comers with ease, or one of the doomed heroes besieging Thebes, taking a beating and slinking with their gear back to wherever they came from.

PLATE 1: Attic Black-figured Panathenaic prize amphora, with two pankratiasts, one holding his opponent in a headlock and about to strike him with his right hand, as the other attempts to free his head; on the left is a contestant with a bye to the next round (*ephedros*), on the right a judge with a forked stick and a wreath, c.332-331BC. British Museum, no.1873,0820.370. Image © The Trustees of the British Museum.

PLATE 2: Attic Black-figured amphora, with two pankratiasts, one with his hand raised in submission; a judge with a forked stick on the left and a bearded figure holding a strap on the right. Attributed to the Leagros Group, c.515-500BC. British Museum, no.1843,1103.69. Image © The Trustees of the British Museum.

PLATE 3: Attic Black-figured Panathenaic prize amphora, with three runners in the *dolichos* (long-distance) race, c.333-332BC. British Museum, no.1856,1001.1. Image © The Trustees of the British Museum.

PLATE 4: Attic Black-figured Panathenaic prize amphora, showing four athletes training rhythmically to music, attributed to Euphiletos Painter, c.530-520BC. British Museum, no.1842,0314.1. Image © The Trustees of the British Museum.

PLATE 5: Attic red-figured stamnos with a muscular Theseus killing the Minotaur: his left arm encircles the Minotaur's neck and grasps its mouth in his left hand, while he steps forward with his left foot on the right shin of his opponent. The Minotaur, blood flowing from his multiple wounds, has fallen backwards onto his right knee; with his right hand he brandishes a stone and with his left he clutches at the left shoulder of Theseus. Attributed to Kleophrades Painter, c.490-480BC. British Museum, no.1866,0805.2. Image © The Trustees of the British Museum.

PLATE 6: Attic red-figured kylix, with two boxers (one with several marks of swelling on his cheek) and two pankratiasts: the one on the left has his right fist poised to deliver a blow while his left arm holds his opponent's head in an armlock, his fingers seeming to claw at his opponent's right eye and the palm and heel of his hand covering his mouth. The opponent has his legs wrapped round the first youth's left leg and he has both hands to that youth's face, thumbs trying to injure or gouge his right eye. On the right a trainer has his forked stick raised to stop foul play. Attributed to Foundry Painter, c.490-480BC. British Museum, no.1850,0302.2. Image © The Trustees of the British Museum.

PLATE 7: Marble metope from the Parthenon sculptures, Athens, showing a Centaur and a Lapith grappling in the Centauromachy. The Lapith has grasped the Centaur by the hair with his right hand, pressing his right knee on the Centaur's breast, and his left arm is drawn back; meanwhile the Centaur, rearing up, seizes the Lapith by the throat, twisting his forelegs round the Lapith's right leg. South Metope no.31, c.437-438BC, designed by Pheidias. British Museum, no.1816,0610.15. Image © The Trustees of the British Museum.

PLATE 8: Attic Black-figured kyathos, showing a crouching Sphinx, c.500 BC, Vatican G57. British Museum, no. 1843,1207.1. Image © The Trustees of the British Museum.

PART TWO:

THE AGON AND THE WORLD

ON THE WORLD STAGE

On the first day of the first week of my training camp for the 2021 Nogi Jiu Jitsu World Championship I popped my knee loud enough for my sparring partner to gasp and cringe and frantically ask if I was alright. In between winces of pain I tried calmly to explain that I was fine; it was the "good" kind of pop. After all, my knees had been popping consistently since I was sixteen, but I knew this one was going to be bad. That pretty much set the tone for the next two months. I had just turned thirty in April of that year, and this would be the first time in my life where the very real, potentially permanent limitations of my body grappled with my innate determination (a nice word I've chosen instead of stubbornness). My knee would continue to pop as I kept training, as I was unwilling to admit I'd been beaten by my own fickle ligaments. I would receive a nasty eye poke about a month later—leaving me severely blurry-eyed for a few days—and a week before the competition I'd shoot for a double-leg, get stuffed, and my foot would fold over on itself, spraining the ligaments (or possibly breaking something; I never went to the doctor).

Was I training like an idiot, recklessly putting myself in risky positions? Probably. As a thirty-year-old full-time PhD student and part-time teacher studying for my qualifying exams while training four-to-five days a week, was I putting a lot of unneeded strain on my mind and body? Most definitely. Why? Because I wanted to win. And not just that, but win big on the world stage. I wanted to feel like I deserved my newly awarded purple belt. I wanted to prove I was more than just a "casual" practitioner. I also wanted the challenge. Preparing for the biggest exams of my life (I would have three days to write three essays, 15 pages each, spanning any number of the 100+ books on my reading list I had been required to read over the preceding semester), I wanted the opportunity to excel in multiple arenas. In other words, I wanted to join the ranks of the ancient Greeks: poets and wrestlers, dancers and boxers, singers and pankratiasts, all of whom sought excellence wherever it could be found. And, if I'm being really honest with myself, I wanted to parade a gold medal in front of my students and the members of my dissertation committee.

The game-plan I chose probably had a lot to do with my frequent injuries. As a relatively small guy, and self-proclaimed guard-pulling leg-locker, I wanted to smash somebody for once. I wanted to wrestle, get the takedown, and put all one-hundred-sixty-two pounds of pressure on my opponent. So that's how I practiced. I refused to pull guard and shot terrible double- and single-legs until it became routine. I sharpened my butterfly and half-guard passes, and would move systematically from half-guard, to mount, to the back, finishing often with a rear-naked-choke. Mike Tyson famously said that "everybody has a plan until they get punched in the face," but in my case, it was more like "everyone has a plan until they step on the mat at Worlds."

Having never been to an IBJJF World Championship before, and having only done one other IBJJF tournament as a white belt, I was awed by the scope of the event. It really was a "world" competition. Checking in to the hotel I brushed elbows with top grapplers. I sipped my morning coffee in the lobby as more streamed in. I watched famous blackbelts eat breakfast across from me at IHOP. It was wild. The confidence I'd been trying to instill in myself was quickly eroding away as the gravity of my situation began to settle in. I was a *very* small fish in a very big ocean. It's true, I was only competing in the Masters purple belt division, but if these were the kinds of blackbelts who turned out, then what caliber of purple belt might be waiting to chew me up and spit me out?

Thankfully I was competing on the second day, so I didn't have long to stew in my own insecurities and fears. I did my best to stay calm, to get good sleep (the latter was almost impossible, as I tossed and turned in my bed for hours). I listened to the smooth ukulele melodies of Jack Johnson's album *In Between Dreams* to try and keep my heart-rate down, and enjoyed the small consolation of eating however much I wanted since I wouldn't be cutting weight (though the nerves made that difficult, a half-finished veggie omelet my only sustenance on the day I would step on the mats).

A brief incident at IHOP of all places on the morning-of strangely set my mind at ease. I was sitting with my mother, picking at my veggie omelet, drinking coffee to compound my jitters, when I looked at the couple sitting at the table directly next to us. I recognized the face of the guy somehow. Where had I seen him? Then it hit me, *he's my first opponent*. I had done my research on the first person I was matched with, and here he was. What were the odds? The whole thing rang as darkly hilarious. Later, before we left, I made the decision to introduce myself and ask for a selfie. He smiled and chuckled, but was clearly taken aback, ultimately agreeing to take a picture (which I proceeded to forward to everyone, along with the story). Having already faced him at the morning IHOP circus, having shaken his hand and talked briefly, a weight of anxiety slipped off my shoulders. Was it the biggest competition of my life? Of course it was. Was it also a little silly that two grown-ass-men with knee pain and adult responsibilities would soon be trying to smother and strangle each other in front of a thousand strangers for the chance to win a five-dollar colored medal and brag about it later on Facebook? One-hundred percent.

The competition itself was like nothing I had planned for or predicted (as so often seems the case). For one, the arena coordinators told me at the door that I had to throw away any outside drinks, so I tossed my two large Gatorades and bottle of water, leaving me without anything to hydrate with after my matches. I got lost in the traffic of competitors and couldn't find the warm-up room, then when it came time to weigh in I realized I'd left my I.D. with my mom (whom I frantically had to flag down in the audience). Finally, I mistook which mat I was supposed to be on and only barely made it in time for my first match.

My plan to wrestle was taken off the table as three of my four opponents immediately pulled guard, and the one who chose to stand with me spectacularly stuffed my poorly attempted double-leg so that I had to desperately try and recover both my position and my dignity. In the end, I won my first three matches (all on points), and lost my final match via submission in the semi-finals. I would take home a bronze, not gold, medal. Having fought for my life much of the time, narrowly escaping several submissions in my second match and clawing to victory with every ounce of energy I had, I was happy to be done with it all—the medal being by then just a nice bonus.

That didn't stop me from bragging about it, of course, and I wore my bulky bronze medal to teach during class the next day, and made much of my accomplishment on social media. All attention-seeking aside, I felt like I'd really done something significant; that even though I hadn't come away with the gold (that honor went to someone who proceeded to get his brown belt on the podium, which made me feel better about myself), I'd validated the belief that I was capable of hanging with some of the best one-hundred-sixty-two pound, thirty-year-old purple belts in the world.

This colorful anecdote had largely to do with a landmark in my own life and competition history, but the whole process of training camp and tournament, of overcoming obstacles to health and strategy, makes me contemplate the ancient Greek athletes who trained and competed at the Olympic Games, who sweated naked in the open under the Mediterranean sun, covered in olive oil and sand, all before the eyes of spectators from their own and every other polis. There were no second or third place medals in such prestigious Panhellenic competitions (no medals at all, in fact—only the olive or laurel wreath—the glory was in their victory alone). You either won, or in the image of Pindar, you would slink home in shame, at night and by back roads.

THE CHIMAERA

Recently I stumbled on a satirical Jiu Jitsu article entitled "Local BJJ Student Receives Blue Belt, Becomes Unholy Chimera of Apex Predators," which struck a number of interesting notes in my mind. First of all, it's hilarious, and anyone who has their blue belt, has progressed past blue belt, or has been training for six months or more, understands exactly why it's hilarious, and can maybe envision particular blue belts in their minds who it might apply to (maybe even themselves). I texted a screenshot to a black belt friend of mine who responded with a deadpan, "He's the most dangerous lion in the ocean," perfectly summarizing the humorous juxtaposition of feeling oneself to be a predator, while in reality being about as menacing as a lion trying to swim. There's nothing quite like explaining a joke to really drive home how funny it is, eh?

The next thing that occurred to me is how *niche* the joke is. I could share the article with any number of my friends who don't train, and their responses would likely vary from sympathetic chuckles to bewildered shoulder shrugs. The idea (and the reality) of the over-inflated ego of the recently promoted blue-belt, or even the significance of the blue belt itself, is utterly lost on folks who haven't already drunk the BJJ Kool-Aid. Brazilian Jiu Jitsu carries with it a particular dialect, or encoded series of linguistic cues, which are only decipherable by those who practice the sport (like an inside joke). This applies equally to the techniques themselves, which are a kind of discourse among training partners, the more adept at "speaking the lingo" of course being the higher belts. But we won't go down the linguistic rabbit hole just yet.

Lastly, being the lover of Greek myth that I am, it's impossible to read the title without the word *Chimera*, also spelled *Chimaera*, with all its implications and associations, punching me right in the nose. Whoever wittily thought of the title clearly knew their mythology too, as *unholy* is one of the most apt adjectives for such a creature.

But for anyone else who isn't a total nerd, here's the gist of the mythology: The Chimaera was a monstrous creature with the body of a lion, whose tail was a snake's head. As if that weren't horrifying enough, protruding from the creature's back was a fire-breathing goat's head, of all things. Needless to say, it was the offspring of two equally horrible monsters, Typhon (the "lawless" and "terrible" who once challenged Zeus for supremacy—and nearly succeeded), and his consort Echidna.[41] It's one of the most fearsome creatures in all of Greek mythology. Our main source of information on the Chimaera comes from Homer's *Iliad*, wherein is described the killing of the beast by the hero Bellerophon, who shot him down while riding the winged horse Pegasus.

But while the mythology behind the Chimaera is interesting in its own right, more interesting still are the various associations which came to be attached to the name. At first, as its meaning developed, it came to represent any hybrid, fictional creature composed of

What could be a better, unironic description of an accomplished mixed martial artist than a Chimaera?

different animal parts. Then gradually it moved away from animals completely, and was associated with anything composed of wildly disparate parts. Finally, it came to mean anything fantastical or wildly imaginative. It's the second definition, *anything* composed of very disparate parts, which is of particular interest for us, and which is closely linked, as the satirical article suggests, to the world of Brazilian Jiu Jitsu and Mixed Martial Arts.

All jokes about blue belts aside, the concept of the Chimaera as related to Brazilian Jiu Jitsu and mixed martial arts is rich with metaphorical possibility, and who better than the ancient Greeks to give it to us? What could be a better, unironic description of an accomplished mixed martial artist than a *Chimaera*? Even the name of the sport lends itself to an association with disparate martial arts, *mixed* together in a precise and threatening combination. Additionally, it is the role of the Chimaera in Greek mythology to be a threat to the established cosmic order, and which combat discipline has been more displacing or demystifying of the established order of martial arts than Brazilian Jiu Jitsu? The gods of Olympus, here represented by sports like boxing, or largely pseudo-martial arts like Tai-Chi or Wing-Chun, have been effectively banished over the course of thirty years since the establishment of the UFC. Who can think of boxing now without thinking of James Toney getting choked out by Randy Couture in the first round of his debut MMA bout after mercilessly attacking mixed martial artists with any number of homophobic slurs? Or traditional martial arts without thinking of the Chinese MMA fighter Xu Xiaodong, who challenged Kung Fu and

Tai Chi "masters" and beat the absolute breaks off them? While the Chimaera never actually displaced the gods of Mount Olympus, this use of the image today only shows the viability of Greek Mythology in contemporary culture, as it is the nature of allegory to be applicable (and at times adaptable) to successive generations.

In this setting, the Chimaera represents versatility and enhanced skills in Mixed Martial Arts and Brazilian Jiu Jitsu. With the body of a wrestler, the legs of a Muay Thai fighter, the hands of a boxer, and the mind of a Jiu Jitero, our modern Chimaera easily attacks and defeats the resistance of each singular discipline, gaining prominence at the top of the combat sport food chain, as well as in our modern consciousness. The old gods have fallen. They are no longer able to possess our culture in the ways they had previously with the movies of Bruce Lee or Jackie Chan except perhaps in the limited experience of our collective suspension of disbelief.

CENTAUROMACHY

At the wedding feast of Pirithous, King of the legendary Lapiths who dwelled in Thessaly, a tribe of Centaurs under the rule of Eurytion became intoxicated on wine, and in a mad drunken dash attempted to make off with the bride of Pirithous. In an instant all were on their feet, both men and Centaurs, and what had previously been a scene of celebration quickly devolved into one of carnage as the two sides tore each other apart. The battle was fierce, with significant losses on both sides, the Lapiths only managing to prevail when the hero Theseus joined their side and darkness fell on the bloody festivities. The Centaurs fled Thessaly into the Peloponnese, leaving their dead behind.

The Centauromachy, as it has come to be known, has provided inspiration for a number of artists and sculptors. In many of them, one can observe the prominence of multiple limbs (understandable, considering the Centaurs had the bodies of horses), and particularly a kind of "hand fighting," or grasping for control over hooves and hands, much like one might find in a modern, or ancient, wrestling match.[42] In one, a Lapith grasps both front hooves, while in another a Centaur rears up, gripping a Lapith by the throat. (See PLATE 7). In yet another, a Centaur holds a Lapith's lower leg in what appears to be a kind of ankle-lock or heel-hook. It seems that a large portion of the fighting was hand-to-hand, or hand-to-hoof.

The common interpretation of this scene as the triumph of civilization over barbarism or human over animalistic

the triumph of grappling over striking

is not without its merits, but for my purposes I think a reinterpretation of the battle through the lens of modern combat sports will yield new and provocative results.

Anyone with even a peripheral knowledge of mixed martial arts who has a glance at the artwork will notice what I've just elaborated upon—the prominence of limbs, either being grasped or being used as offensive weapons—and it wouldn't be an enormous leap in logic to assume that eventually they might make the connection between the Centauromachy and pankration, i.e. our ancient iteration of mixed martial arts: the combined use of kicks, punches, and grappling for maximum damage output. In other words, an all-out wedding brawl made up of numerous individual *agones* was the first mythological instance of what many of us practice on the mats today.

I've spent time interpreting the metaphorical significance of multi-limbed monsters in other chapters, but here again we have another instance—the six-limbed Centaurs on the one hand have a plethora of weapons available to them, while on the other they have an equal number of potential targets for a brave and skilled Lapith to grab hold of. It's worth taking some time to analyze these hybrid creatures in this light, as well as the advantages of their counterparts the Lapiths. Lapiths and Centaurs were in fact genealogically connected in myth, each tribe being descended from twin sons of Apollo and a river-nymph.

Several years ago, the Jiu Jitsu wizard and leg-lock aficionado John Danaher was a guest on Joe Rogan's podcast to talk primarily about, well, Jiu Jitsu. Besides his looking like a lizard in his green-scaled rash guard, I remember a particularly interesting discussion the two had on the nature of Jiu Jitsu's effectiveness in combat sports. It involved four principles, all coldly related by Danaher to the rapt and attentive Rogan. They are as follows: 1. Take the fight to the ground, 2. Pass the legs, 3. Secure position, and 4. Apply submission (breaking or choking). These principles seem obvious enough in light of the nature of the sport (Jiu Jitsu takes place on the ground, after all, so it only makes sense to take the fight there), but what I find most interesting is Danaher's physiological justification for *why* the fight must be taken to the ground, and *why*, in order to secure position and finish a submission, one must first get past the opponent's legs.

In the podcast episode, Danaher explains the principle of kinetic energy, and the enormous potential of a person's legs and hips to generate that energy, particularly when striking (for anyone familiar with boxing, they will understand that the majority of our punching power actually comes from the rotation of the hips). Therefore, he concludes, a person's ability to deliver maximum striking force will necessarily take place while they are in a standing position. As a result, by taking the fight to the ground, one is able to substantially eliminate the amount of energy able to be delivered in a single strike. Once the fight is on the ground, the legs of one's opponent are still dangerous, able to deliver what are referred to as "up-kicks" which can have a devastating impact if landed cleanly. Hence, Danaher's second principle of Jiu Jitsu is to "pass the legs." Once this is done, the ability of a grappler to manipulate their opponents is greatly increased, and the likelihood of submission all but guaranteed.

Returning to the physiology of the Centaurs, and based on John Danaher's principles, it makes perfect sense to assume that the potential kinetic energy they are able to produce is exponential in relation to their human counterparts. The Centaurs present a formidable obstacle, indeed. In many of the stone reliefs depicting the wedding debacle, the Centaurs appear to be getting the better of the Lapiths, at least in the hand-to-hand combat aspect of the fighting. The Centaurs can be seen with the Lapiths in various choke holds, or with their front hooves in the air, poised to strike, with various weapons, even boulders. Interestingly, in many of the depictions one can see a Lapith "mounting" the back of a Centaur, a single knee forcing the beast to the ground, with his front hooves kneeling in the dirt. Having thus passed by the dangerous limbs and taken the back of his opponent, the Lapith is free to deliver a killing blow.

One of the great exceptions to Danaher's principles are the leglocks which have gained prominence recently in the Jiu Jitsu world, and which we even see in some of the ancient portrayals of the Centauromachy. While the first principle remains the same, that the fight must be taken to the ground (though this is not *always* the case), rather than passing the legs one is able to grab hold of a leg in order to apply any number of submissions (kneebar, heel hook, ankle lock etc.). We have images of Lapiths fighting from the ground (usually in some trouble), but it's easy to imagine one taking control of a Centaur's leg and applying some kind of submission, whether an ankle lock or a heel hook, and in this regard the Centaurs are particularly vulnerable where they have previously been superior (their striking power coming from their many legs). Here we'd have an instance of taking an opponent's apparent strength and turning it against them, with devastating results, something very common in Jiu Jitsu. There is a well-known depiction of the reverse, a Centaur who has taken control of the leg of a Lapith sprawled on the ground and is in a position to go for a heel-hook and another showing an arm-lock.[43]

Returning to the more traditional interpretation of the Centauromachy as the triumph of civilization over barbarism, we can equally apply a modern interpretation through the lens of combat sports. For many years, prior to the Gracie family's United States expansion and the inception of the UFC, it was popularly held that striking disciplines were superior to grappling. More "manly," more "honorable" and other epithets were applied to various striking sports, especially with the dissemination of Kung Fu, Wing Chun, Karate, and others in film and popular culture by figures like Bruce Lee and Jackie Chan.

Once the Gracie family began to introduce Brazilian Jiu Jitsu into the popular consciousness (especially after Royce choked out the competition in the first few UFCs), the tides began to change in favor of the grappling arts, and myths of striking superiority were slowly eroded in the light of the hard evidence provided by televised mixed martial arts events. In this light I maintain that, like the Centauromachy, the triumph of grappling (Lapiths) over striking (the Centaurs), represented civilization's triumph over barbarism. Less simplistically, and perhaps more fairly to the striking arts, when the event is taken as a whole, the combination of striking and grappling in the artwork can be interpreted as an artistic expression of mixed martial arts in Greek mythology and culture at large.

CATASTROPHE

The ancient Greek play *Oedipus Rex*, or *Oedipus the King*, written by Sophocles around 429 B.C., chronicles the famous (or infamous) rise and fall of the eponymous Oedipus, king of Thebes, and is arguably the best and best-known of all Greek plays—thanks in large part to its adoption by psychoanalyst Sigmund Freud as an archetype of male sexual development, though we're going to cut a wide path around that can of worms. It's a wild ride from start to finish, and is eminently readable and watchable, even to a modern audience: its themes of fate vs. free-will, pride vs. humility, and sight vs. blindness are rich fare for the English professor, the philosopher, and yes, even the combat athlete. It's no surprise then that the story is filled with conflict, from Oedipus' killing of his father (then unknown to him) in an outburst of road-rage at the crossroads, to his solving the riddle of the Sphinx, to his fierce argument with the prophet Tiresias, to the ultimate revelation of his true identity and the nature of his deeds (*spoiler alert* he gouges his own eyes out and his mother/wife kills herself).

Implicit in the play's action are a series of decisions made by Oedipus—some rash and foolhardy, some clever and brave—which lead him to his final disaster, and, amid the wreckage, self-awareness. It's those decisions, and their metaphorical implications which I believe hold special significance for the combat athlete, and most especially for those who train Brazilian Jiu Jitsu. Themes of sight and blindness have already been developed by

the pinnacle of challenge for anyone brave or foolish enough to attempt

us, so the most significant of these instances for our purposes is the encounter Oedipus' has with the Sphinx outside the city of Thebes.

Before the play begins, Oedipus approaches the city of Thebes and confronts the Sphinx, a monstrous creature with the head and breasts of a woman, the body of a lion, and the wings of an eagle. (See PLATE 8). The name means "Strangler" or Binder" (in the sense of spell-binding or enchanting). This hybrid creature has been terrorizing the inhabitants of the city, devouring any travelers who could not solve its riddle. Oedipus is able to solve the riddle, to break free from the stranglehold, and the Sphinx throws itself from a cliff (some sources say Oedipus killed it with his own hands), thus ending the threat to the city. In gratitude to their savior, the inhabitants of Thebes proclaim Oedipus king and give him in marriage to the dowager-queen Jocasta, and it's after all this that Sophocles' play actually begins. If the significance isn't obvious already, it will be soon enough.

The combat athlete is presented with a number of unique predicaments in training, the most immediate of which is the opponent (whether in training or competition) currently trying to "kill" them. As the athlete progresses in training, the sophistication with which he or she approaches this predicament increases. The match is a kind of discourse between combatants, the more adept claiming ultimate victory. In other words, the opponent is a riddle, and solving or failing to solve that riddle will mean the difference between life or death (metaphorically speaking). Get it now?

The Sphinx wasn't only an obstacle to be overcome; just another trial for the hero to prove his mettle. Rather, the Sphinx was symbolic of anything intellectually and physically threatening; the pinnacle of challenge for anyone brave or foolish enough to attempt. The Sphinx itself was a riddle. In Mixed Martial Arts, there is always a Sphinx to be faced: someone in the running for GOAT status: whether it's Royce Gracie, Anderson Silva, or more recently, Jon Jones, these figures represent the final obstacle standing in the way of the fighter and their goal (or gold), a physical and mental riddle to be solved.

Oedipus is a warrior, having previously trained, fought, and killed opponents with his own hands (notably, his father and his guards). But what separates him from Joe-Schmoe-Greek-Hero is the versatility of his skill set in defeating opponents who approach him with different challenges. He's not a brawler only, but a strategist, rhetorician, and problem-solver. It's for this reason I believe he serves as another archetype of contemporary mixed martial artists.

And while it is perhaps only coincidental, there is an interesting parallel between the posture of the Sphinx and that of its modern-day human equivalents in the Octagon. Take for instance the crouching position it assumes, poised, ready to strike (making clear the threat this opponent poses if he fails to solve the riddle)—then take as a parallel image the well-known crouching posture of Jon Jones before the bell rings for round one. The two are nearly the same. The positional confidence of the apex predator spans both time and place.

In a recent interview with the UFC fighter Valentina Shevchenko, former fighter Michael Bisping asked Shevchenko, then one of the most dominant female fighters in UFC history, if she was taking her opponent for granted or if she had prepared for the advanced skillset she might face in her bout. Shevshenko replied, "I know where I am weakest, and I intend to avoid being put into those positions." Her response displayed the kind of responsible self-knowledge which Oedipus lacked, and suffered catastrophically for by the end of the play. Oedipus' tragic flaw of arrogant self-assurance catches up to him, and disaster befalls the once mighty king in the form of various revelations—that in his fury he had killed his real father, and had married his biological mother. All of history is witness to his fall. He pursued the advice of the Greek maxim, *Gnothi seauton* (Know Thyself, i.e., know who and what you truly are) with relentless drive, but was ultimately crushed by the truth which emerged.

The word "catastrophe" comes to us—surprise, surprise—from the Greek. Its root words are *kata*, meaning down, and *strophe*, a kind of turning, and it originates in the overturning of a chariot during a race or being thrown down for a fall in wrestling. The word over time developed into a description of any great and sudden disaster, which can be applied readily to a sudden change of fate in a fight or in training. Greek dramatists had a term for the exact moment when this "turn of fate" or "reversal of fortune" occurs: *peripeteia*.

Anyone who has trained is familiar with this phenomenon, and the longer one trains the more painfully familiar one becomes with it. It can take many forms: the devastating blast-double or Harai Goshi, the reversal via any number of sweeps from bottom position (a literal overturning), or the sudden and surprising submission. One's response to this catastrophe depends on their level of training, their *foresight*, let's say. But to a degree catastrophes are inevitable, and no amount of preparation can prevent them. Here the Oedipus analogy falls apart somewhat (pun intended), as Oedipus was *fated* for a fall, preceded as he was by prophesies of catastrophe. Fighters can choose their own destiny to an extent, and their reactions depend entirely on both their training and state of mind—for example, whenever someone lands a clean technique, especially if it was obvious and I fail to realize it, I usually can't help but laugh out loud at my own stupidity or their skill. What this says about me I'm not entirely sure, though I do immediately get back to work in improving my position. In the context of Greek tragedy, the *peripeteia* and *katastophe* are followed by *anagnorisis*, meaning "recognition" or "realization."

Combat sports are unique in relation to drama (Greek drama especially), in that the sudden catastrophes can take place immediately, without the necessary plot development or character arch present in traditional narratives. This catastrophe is usually the most unexpected and entertaining, as it involves a devastating knock-out or flashy flying submission of some kind (numerous examples exist, but my more recent favorites are Tyron Woodley's knockout of Robbie Lawler and Ryan Hall's Imanari Roll-heel hook finish of BJ Penn). Likewise in ancient Greek combat sports, before signals of submission became standard in boxing and pankration, even wrestling had a kind of dramatic arc which differs from some contemporary bouts, requiring as it did a total of three falls to achieve victory (rather than a sudden unforeseen victory). But catastrophe in the Octagon isn't always the norm (in fact, more often than not the result is foreseen in the dominance of one opponent over another over the course of three rounds), and the drama of a fight plays out in many similar ways to Greek drama, especially when the fight has been highly touted in the media, or takes place between rivals. Everyone gathers to watch the moment when the sudden reversal of fortune occurs, and what brings it about.

What I think the story of Oedipus ultimately teaches combat athletes is the value of foresight and humble anticipation of catastrophe, but barring that, the athlete's ability to recover, to reflect and change. While not present in the original play, in its sequel *Oedipus at Colonus*, the reader finds an older, blind, yet wiser Oedipus, living in poverty and exile with his daughters Antigone and Ismene. While he still possesses many of the qualities of pre-blind Oedipus, he nevertheless exhibits restraint and reflection, a clear departure from his previous unrelenting pride. Likewise, the combat athlete, even perhaps the young and arrogant up-and-comers in the sport, or those yet to experience serious competitive setbacks, must necessarily grow from inevitable catastrophe (for catastrophe is *always* inevitable), or else lapse into the exile of prideful self-deception and the diminishing of their faculties.

SPECTATORS

Even the most peripheral fans of sports are likely familiar with the effect a roaring crowd of spectators can have on an athlete's performance, and it's no great mental stretch to imagine the impact on athletes in combat sports as being even greater still. After all, for those athletes fighting in the cage, it's not a missed field goal or three pointer they have to worry about (or the ire of annoyed and drunken fans), but their immediate physical well-being.

During the COVID pandemic the lack of spectators in the arena led to an eerie hollow silence accompanying the thwap of a landed leg kick or flush right hand. Another, perhaps more thorough study of crowd effects might gauge the difference it made on the mental state of the athletes—whether or not they were able to concentrate better with fewer distractions from the heckling crowd—but speaking more personally, as a fan and student of the sport, it was a relief to be able to narrow my focus to the fighters, along with the knowledgeable commentary of Rogan and Co.

Fighting sports in particular suffer from an overwhelming number of backseat fighters: people (mostly men) with little-to-no experience of actual training or fighting, convinced they have the magic combination for an easy and brutal knockout which will be sure to garner the fighter immortality, as well as a nice 50k performance bonus from Dana White. Of course, anyone who has ever trained or fought knows it's not so simple. As one of my old boxing coaches used to tell me, there's a reason it's called *boxing* and not *hitting*. If it were as easy as willing oneself to land a highlight reel technique every second of every match, then even the most undisciplined among us would be title contenders.

Years ago, when satirical news outlet *The Onion* was still relevant, they released an article entitled "Report: Average Male 4000% Less Effective in Fights Than They Imagine," and though I'd read it before I ever started training, it stuck in my mind (and of course now it's far funnier to me). Maybe it's testosterone, or some leftover impulse of evolution, or a case of Natty Lite—or maybe it's the nature of fighting in general—but for whatever reason combat sports tickle the ego and obsesses the male brain more than any other. Interestingly though, with that obsession comes a corresponding lethargy when it comes to actually learning *how* to fight (of course this same lethargy was the underlying target of the *Onion* article).

A family friend once hosted a "ninja" themed birthday for one of their younger kids, and they asked me to come and teach a short Jiu Jitsu lesson to the crowd of toddlers. I did, and it went as expected (half deserted immediately, while the other half stood around absently kicking rocks), but what was most interesting was the response from the dads of the group. A number came up to me to "talk shop," so to speak, about their experience (or lack thereof), and one in particular stands out even now. He expressed an interest in learning self-defense, and asked me the best way to go about it. Of course, I explained it wasn't as easy as mastering the Five Point

Palm Exploding Heart Technique, or taking the occasional Krav Maga class—that it takes years of discipline and dedication, requiring at least three days a week of attendance at a reputable Jiu Jitsu or MMA gym (no, I explained, Tai Chi in the park doesn't count). And then, like magic, the excuses started rolling in: "I've got a bad back," "I've got a busy schedule," "I prefer lifting weights," etc.… to which I just nodded and made my exit, thinking to myself, *Well then, you should probably just buy a gun if you're worried about self-defense.*

Now, though it's a slight digression, and the point of this chapter isn't to examine the hang-ups people have with fighting; for a proper comparison to the ancients it's important to set up a proper dichotomy with our contemporary moment. To return to the topic of informed vs. uninformed spectators, it's interesting to me then to offer up the example of a trained observer. While the casual, raucous UFC spectator might yell inanities like "Just knock him out!" or "Stand 'em up, ref!" the experience I've had with my training buddies while watching fights is that we are (typically) collectively silent (though like everyone else we do burst out uproariously when the lights-out blow is landed). Obsessed with technique, and informed to one degree or another, our attention is drawn not so much to the spectacle (the blood and brutality of it all—though that's certainly fun too), as the execution of the *discipline* in real-time. After all, what's the point of fighting if you never get to try it out? And combat sports are the closest (and safest) example we have of *real*, yet contained, violence. In our excitement or egotism, we may offer the occasional prediction or advice—if someone's locked up a kimura from half guard, a sweep is likely to follow; if someone keeps circling to their opponent's power hand, a knockout is coming, etc.... but for the most part, a respect for the gravity of the spectacle holds our tongues.

But our contemporary moment offers an interesting intersectional window through which we can observe the differences between ancient Greek and Roman audiences, and how the phenomena of spectating continue to evolve, devolve, or a combination of both, from one century to another.

For the Greeks, who admittedly dwelled in much smaller communities than our contemporary ones, training in the palaestra was mandatory for male citizens (yes, slaves, women, or non-citizens were generally excluded), and that entire subsection of the population, whether young or old, were informed in all manner of competition, the majority of which related to combat (most would probably have fought as hoplites in their lives, given the frequency of war among city-states). And considering the majority of spectators at an athletic competition between or within city-states were the free adult male citizens, the nature of the spectacle, at least as far as the audience was concerned, was most likely in line with the example I've given of an informed audience enraptured by the execution of technique and skill. The spectacle was more communal, and therefore more intimate and connected to one's self, one's daily life, and one's past or present experience training in the palaestra. When the ancient Greek audience watched a wrestling, boxing, or pankration event, they were watching their friends, neighbors, relatives, and maybe even their training partners compete for the ultimate prize. It may be true that familiarity at other times breeds contempt, but in the realm of combat sports, it breeds respect.

It's worth noting, too, that the spectating audience, as well as the physical characteristics of the combat arena itself, were largely similar for both combat sports and theatrical drama in ancient Greece. Crowds of citizens would be well-versed in the competitive drama of wrestling bouts, and likewise in the metaphorical grappling among gods and heroes of the stage, as the city itself grappled with the practical issues of self-government.

Contrasted with the Greek audience we have spectators in the Roman amphitheater, who more closely resemble the unruly crowds I've already elaborated upon. Larger, more extravagant, and mostly for the purpose of entertainment and distraction, the Roman arena stands in contrast to the intimate familiarity of the ancient Olympics, and therefore appealed to an entirely different constituency. Additionally, as a result of the largely armed spectacles (gladiators and the like), the arena appealed to the fantastical imaginations of its audience, and further emphasized the divide between the trained and untrained, between the warriors fighting in the sand and the audience lounging comfortably in the stands above them. It's worth noting there were no "arenas" in ancient Greece, and the spectators were all largely on the same level as the athletes, as opposed to the tiered "stadium" seating of the Roman arena (think of the Colosseum in the center of imperial Rome), marking out significant physical and social divisions among the people (even though women, slaves and foreigners could generally attend the spectacles).

Returning to our contemporary time, among the crowds of spectators there are cohabitant Greeks and Romans, so to speak—a hodgepodge intermingling and feeding off one another, with the hope at least that the intimate appreciation of informed observers might rub off on the beer-swilling brutes (the stereotypes are largely for laughs, as I'm also a big fan of cheap beer and being brutish). And of course, more positively speaking, modern combat sports have leveled the playing field, allowing those previously excluded groups in ancient Greece a place at the table with equal consideration and information. It's never been a better time to be a spectator, whether Greek or Roman.

TROPHIES

One of the better and more minor problems I've had in recent years has been deciding how exactly to display the increasing number of tournament medals I've won. For a while I had the few I'd won hanging off a mantle, then as they increased I draped them on a shelf, then finally, lacking anything immediately at hand, I stuffed them in a box. It was my mother's idea (and her keen eye for decorating) when I moved into my most recent house to hang them from a wooden ladder she'd found at some department store or other. So now, in my living room, there is a decorative ladder hanging against the wall with two dozen or so medals of various colors draped from each of the rungs. It's nothing crazy, and certainly nothing to feel overly proud about, but for me it serves as a nice reminder of the many times I've competed, along with the stories which accompany them.

From Super Bowl rings to Olympic medals, to the hollowed-out skulls of our enemies, humans have a historical appetite for victory, and rewarding that struggle with trophies. Whether it's the desire for immortality (the still-preserved Roman columns and arches are, after all, a type of trophy), a kind of cathartic claim on an enemy's body (in the form of scalps, for instance), a reminder of past victories, or simply a visual display of bragging rights, it's safe to say that the taking and bestowing of trophies has been common across civilizations.

Ancient Greeks set up a trophy (*tropaion*) on the battlefield, marking the place where the battle "turned" (*trope*) in their favor when the enemy's phalanx fell apart and they were routed. Thucydides describes the trophy as a celebration of the killing of the enemy and a notification of their defeat in battle. The *tropaion* was originally a tree, whose branches would be decorated with hoplite weaponry and shields, helmets and other items would be piled up around its roots. A tree of all natural objects would be best suited for displaying the armor of fallen enemies for all to see.

Until I discovered Brazilian Jiu Jitsu and began competing in earnest, the majority of my accolades were comprised of participation trophies from consistently unsuccessful adolescent baseball teams, the 2nd or 3rd place ribbons from track meets and cross-country races, or even, on one occasion, a towering first-place trophy I received purely as a result of belonging to a youth basketball team with better players who were not me.

As pathetic as my youthful athletic accomplishments were, it seemed at first slightly more pathetic to be a grown-ass man competing in a combat sport of all things. In my first tournament I paid $80 to scrape by with a single victory and claim a $2 silver medal. Hardly compelling material for an after-school special—especially considering I had an immediate adrenaline dump and barely survived, spending the entire match on bottom, scrambling for guard, just managing to toss up a triangle before I completely gassed out. But like training, competing takes practice, and as I began to compete more

and more, my confidence grew, along with my medal count (though my sense of absurdity at what had become a serious passion never really left).

Now, having something like fifteen tournaments under my belt (pun intended), two dozen or so medals (the majority of which are gold, though with a fair amount of silver and bronze mixed in), and having suffered a number of competition-related injuries, I can safely say this obsessive and often ridiculous striving after trophies has tremendously enriched my life.

I say enriched, and I mean it, though it has been for entirely unexpected reasons. In the musically inspired fantasy montages running through my mind early in my competition "career," I envisioned myself highlight-reeling one poor bastard after another, climbing the ranks of competitors like the Mortal Kombat ladder, all the way to the top. I practiced my Imanari Roll and Harai Goshi, hoping to be able to put it to good use in a tournament (preferably while someone was filming), and it's worth noting that on the rare occasion I dared the flashier techniques, they *always* backfired, often horrendously—including one such occasion in the absolute division when my Imanari Roll against a 240 lbs. opponent was squashed, as he countered it by simply sitting down on me. In reality, many of my wins have come from entirely unspectacular basic techniques which are still a source of embarrassment whenever I peruse the unfortunate video evidence. And if it isn't a result of basic technique it's simply my ability to *outlast* my opponent, weathering the storm of attacks until they're too exhausted to continue.

Again, hardly material for a movie like *Remember the Titans*.

But if the enrichment of competition hasn't been a result of my overwhelming victories, highlight-reel techniques, or sheer barbaric onslaught against my opponents, then why have I insisted on its indispensable value in my life? I'll explain with an example from my second tournament.

When I was training in Boone, NC, an associate of our gym organized a small local tournament in the town of Kingsport, TN. Because it was so small, the weight-classes were divided in two: under 170 and over 170. That's it. At barely 155 lbs., I wasn't thrilled about the possibility of fighting opponents that much bigger than me, but I wanted to support my gym and signed up anyway. My first round was, predictably, against a larger man. I decided I'd pull guard and work off my back, which was at that time my strongest attacking position. When I managed to trap him in a pre-triangle position (without the arm yet across or my legs locked up appropriately), he immediately began to stack me hard, folding me over on myself almost to the point where my knees touched my nose. I felt a ripping sensation in my side, and then heard a popping sound followed by horrible pain. I'd dislocated one of my ribs within a minute and a half of the first round.

Somehow, I managed to survive through to the overtime rounds (it was an EBI inspired tournament, so we were placed in different positions after the initial time had expired), and submitted my opponent with a rear-naked choke. In the time between matches I approached my coach and told him what had happened, wincing at what was an entirely new pain sensation. He asked if I wanted to continue, telling me there'd be no shame in backing out. I paused, thinking seriously on his offer to throw in the towel and replied with "Fuck it, I didn't drive all the way out here just to lose." It was one of the decisions of which I'm most proud. I went on to beat two more opponents, all while severely limited in my ability to maneuver. I claimed first place in my division. Because it was a small local tournament, the trophy was cheaply made, as was the medal I received. And yet, these maintain a prominent place in my collection, higher even than the bronze medal I later won at the IBJJF Nogi World Championship.

The wins over my opponents in those matches were anything but spectacular. I probably looked like a wounded animal just barely managing to get the better of its predators (thankfully, no video evidence exists), and yet, it was the spirit of perseverance, the grit it took to continue fighting, which I'm most proud of. It's my victories as an underdog which take prominence on my medal stand. And that I think is the heart of competition and its rewards: the testing, not necessarily of one's technical abilities (though that is certainly part of it), but, to use that horrible cliché, of one's *heart*—the Greeks had so much better words, like *thumos* or *menos*, as we saw earlier. When the chips are down (another cliché), when you're tired or injured, how do you react? I've won gold medals with minimal effort, and I've worked my ass off for bronze. You can guess which mean more to me.

As we have discussed, the ancient Greeks weren't exempt from the competitive spirit. In fact, every aspect of their culture was permeated with it (I would even argue their society was a *paragon* of competition). If there was a potential for perfection, the Greeks strove and competed for it, often besting each other in arranged bouts along the way. And it wasn't athletics only, but the arts as well—the best of Greek drama was originally composed for poetic "tournaments" between three prominent playwrights in Athens. The great Panhellenic competitions like the Olympia were rooted in religious and historical significance and the prestige of winning the victor's crown of olive leaves cannot be exaggerated.

Today's medals are ultimately derived from this practice, although the separation into gold, silver and bronze began with the revival of the Olympic Games in 1896. Even here, though, there is a Greek precedent: the Great Panathenaic festival in Athens, with its array of musical and athletic competitions, including some "team" events like relay-races, did have prizes for second and third, sometimes for fourth and fifth places too. That, however, is something of an exception as the festival's primary focus was the fostering of civic pride among Athenians, citizens of the remarkable *polis* that would become the template for democracy in Greece as well as the hub of artistic creativity.

And while it's impossible to know for certain the motivations of each competitor, some of the most famous examples of victory come from anecdotes where the odds were stacked against one of the opponents who ultimately triumphed in spite of the odds. Everyone loves an underdog. This gives us reason to believe that while winning was of highest importance, it was an even greater triumph to possess the superior spirit and will to achieve victory in the face of adversity. Hence the Greeks imagined victory as *Nike* (yes, it's the same word as the brand), a winged maiden who flies through the air and rests on high (often in the hands of Zeus or Athena)—and is especially difficult to grasp.

And so ultimately, for the Greeks, for us, and for everybody in-between, trophies signify far more than potential immortality or the entirely deserved accolades of our respective city-states (or the over-admiring white belts in the gym)—it gratifies a necessity inherent in the human spirit to prove oneself against adversity; to rise to the occasion, with or against the odds. It signifies to the competitor (the first, last, and most important critic) the value of their training and strength of their character.

NO WALLS AT SPARTA

What is it about combat sports in general, and Brazilian Jiu Jitsu in particular, that appeals as a *deterrent* for excessive aggression? This seems a bit contradictory, since the nature of combat sports is, well, combative, yes? Combative sports are combative—surprise, surprise—but it's perhaps *actually* surprising to the casual observer, or the untrained, how effective consistent training in combat sports is at preventing unrestrained or unwarranted aggression in its practitioners.

When I'm back home in Charleston there's a Checkmat gym where I like to train. Everyone's welcoming, the technique is solid, and the rolls are competitive. I enjoy the gym so much I recommended it to my brother, and now his two sons train there five days a week. Interestingly, the gym is located in a long-defunct strip mall which used to be a single grocery store, so none of the now separate businesses are distinct save for their individual signs. And who happens to be the next-door neighbor to Checkmat? Gold's Gym. Equally interesting, and unique to any gym where I've trained, the only "wall" dividing the two gyms is a window so members from either place can peer through to see what the others are up to. This unique partition has resulted in a symbiotic relationship between the two—members from Checkmat do their lifting and showering at Gold's, and the Gold's has fed consistent white belts into the Jiu Jitsu meat grinder of Checkmat.

In Sparta—unlike Athens, or any other ancient city for that matter—there were no walls to protect from invaders. Having achieved a nearly-mythic reputation for invincibility in the field of combat, there seemed little need. If an opponent wanted to try their strength, just let them, and may the best city-state win. The wall-less mentality of the Spartans reflects not only their martial confidence, but likewise their willingness to accept the possibility of defeat. We're all likely familiar with the aphorism made popular by the film *300*, "Come back with your shield or on it," attributed to the Spartans. The admittedly limited options of victory or death nevertheless allow for a strange freedom—freedom from fear of the shame of defeat, of enslavement, of death, and therefore freedom from the need for protection beyond the strength of one's own arm.

This wall-less mentality is reflected in the most successful Jiu Jitsu gyms. In an ideal training environment, there are no walls to knowledge, nor is there anything to hide behind; the instructor is no different than the first-day white belt in that they are both exposed to the possibility of "death" on the mats. Likewise, anyone is able to walk in off the streets and train like a member of the team, bringing their own expertise to the melting pot of the mats. No technique is "off-limits" or walled off, so to speak, and even if it is strange or unorthodox, if it works it's up for grabs.

In ancient Greece, each free male citizen was required to be enrolled from a young age in a rigorous training regimen, which included instruction in weapons and tactics, boxing, wrestling, running and other athletics, as well as singing, dancing, poetry, and philosophy. This instruction was paramount for their development into flourishing, productive citizens, implicit in which was their viability as soldiers on the battlefield. The ability to defend their families and city-states, especially in the turbulent era rife with domestic warfare and foreign invasions, was their first priority. And of all training regimens, none was tougher than the Spartan *agoge*, designed to produce invincible soldiers.

Anyone who's seen the movie *300*—a flamboyant, highly exaggerated, slo-mo recounting of the doomed Spartan defense of Thermopylae—will perhaps remember the first scene of battle joined between the undisciplined Persian hordes, rushing haphazardly and headlong, and the tightly formed ranks of Spartan defenders waiting for them. What I remember most about that scene aren't the flexed Spartan abs, the ridiculous battlefield chatter, or even the terrible CGI blood bursts, but rather the overwhelming clamor of the initial crashing wave of Persians against Spartan shields—where, for a brief moment, the defenders seemed overmatched and overwhelmed by the sheer number of attackers, pushed back several feet from their initial positions. But then there's the nonchalance of the Spartans which immediately deflates any tension or foreboding. The bemuscled Greeks laugh and joke behind their locked shields, and as we the audience guessed all along, soon rally behind coordinated thrusts with spear and shield, scattering the bewildered ranks of the enemy all the way to the nearby cliffs.

Seeing the movie in the theater, the effect of that initial clash was all the more jarring, and perhaps I'm not alone in imagining my own response to such overwhelming stimuli. Of course, who wouldn't hope they'd be among the laughers and jokesters of the group? There is a sneaking suspicion in me, however, that I'd be one of the silent few, terrified and untested. While there is certainly no substitute for actual combat experience, the training experienced in combat sports gyms, especially the inevitable overwhelming claustrophobia of Jiu Jitsu, seems to me the closest imitation of those sensations. But with consistent imitation comes a certain level of familiarity with the uncomfortable or terrifying, and it's this nullification of panic which I think was one of the main motivators behind the rigorous training regimen in the *agoge* and other schools of combat instruction in ancient Greece.

And it wasn't for those purposes only, but for the unification of their young men in a single unit. Combat sports, ironically even more so than team sports, requires a strong bond of trust between training partners. If I'm rolling, I have to be able to trust that my partner will honor the tap if they're lucky enough to catch me, and of course vice versa. The same was obviously true for the Greeks, and even more so as they were practicing at times with more than just their bodies, but with sword and spear and shield. The trust, both implicit and actively fostered among their ranks, combined of course with the nature of their closely-packed phalanx formation, allowed their armies to face down even the most overwhelming odds with poise and calm. This was the bond underpinning the success of the hoplite phalanx in battle against much larger forces (in the case of the invading Persians), but also against similar armies from other Greek cities. It was further strengthened in Sparta by rigorous training from childhood in the *agoge* and by uniquely close attachments formed by pairs of fighters in the so-called Theban Band, an elite unit organized and trained by the military genius Epaminondas, which ultimately enabled the city of Thebes to achieve the unimaginable—routing the hitherto undefeated Spartans at the Battle of Leuctra in 371BC and shattering their myth of invincibility.

It should come as no surprise then why combat training has gained popularity among those who face physical dangers in their daily occupation—the ability to remain calm in the most stressful situations humans might encounter being among one of the most valuable skills they could possess. Like the Greeks before them, our modern armed and unarmed response forces benefit from consistent combat sports training. But the benefits of self-possession aren't reserved for those who encounter the most stressful situations on a daily basis, they are also for casual practitioners like me.

Growing up I wasn't encouraged in my physicality—fighting was discouraged, even in self-defense—and because I was small, I suffered from poor physical confidence for the majority of my life until I found boxing, and ultimately, Brazilian Jiu Jitsu. Confidence and composure under pressure are two of the main reasons why I continue to train (getting to legally strangle and maim your friends isn't too bad either).

Starting out in combat sports, my first exposure was with boxing, and I trained exclusively for about nine months before starting Brazilian Jiu Jitsu. Recently, I took up striking again, hoping to shake off the rust a bit, and after a particularly hard sparring session, afterwards feeling the familiar incipient headache and fuzziness, I wondered why I'd bothered putting myself through the more immediately painful learning curves of striking all over again. The answers penetrated even the growing fog of a minor concussion.

Although of course I'm no accomplished striker, and at 33 have no plans of trying my luck in the Octagon, the importance of being able to throw hands (or feet) in the unlikely event of a self-defense scenario can't be overstated. Besides being able to set up potential takedowns with a solid jab, the ability to read body language, and especially a telegraphed punch (or kick), could be essential for being able to take charge of an altercation and put a swift stop to it.

Along with that, there is always the potential in a street fight you will take some sort of damage (there's always a "puncher's chance" as they say), and in that case, I for one would rather be as acclimated to taking damage as possible, hence getting punched in the face repeatedly at practice—and, of course, being a sub-par striker gives one plenty of opportunities for that.

Lastly, the ability to control oneself in extremely stressful situations is possibly the most important of all the qualities which striking practice can give. For anyone who has experienced an adrenaline dump and the extreme fatigue which follows, knows how dangerous it could potentially be if one were in real danger. Therefore, the ability to regulate one's adrenaline and breathing might potentially make the critical difference in who walks away unharmed.

And speaking of adrenaline regulation, competing is another way of acclimating oneself to the fight or flight impulse—and of course that doesn't mean going out and signing up for a boxing tournament on a whim like I did (though it was great experience, even if I didn't get that highlight reel knockout I was hoping for). I for one hate competing, though I do love winning. I hate the weight cut, the stress of anticipation, and the chance that after all the effort put into the process, I might not walk away with anything to show for it. It is a wholly uncomfortable experience for me, and it's exactly for that reason I consistently force myself to compete in tournaments, at the local, national, and occasional world level. It's that discomfort which grows up in me that very acclimation which might one day serve me well in a street fight, and which has already served me in more minor stressful situations. Every time I have to present at a conference, I tell myself, "At least no one is trying to strangle me or punch me in the face," and it works!

And so Jiu Jitsu, boxing, Muay Thai, and the like aren't only for the front-lines of stress and anxiety, but can be equally applicable to wannabe-badasses like myself and others, whose only battlefields may be speaking in public or telling the occasional obnoxious movie-goer to pipe down.

THE GOLDEN FLEECE

The first time I watched the 1963 film *Jason and the Argonauts*, I was probably seven or eight years old. There was a small video rental store (back when those existed) down the road from my house, and I was allowed every weekend to pick out a handful of videotapes (yes, you read that correctly—videotapes, the kind you had to rewind) to watch on my own while my mom and dad worked. I don't remember what else I chose that night, but I remember distinctly the scenes depicted on its covers, with pictures on the back of stop-motion skeletons, bearded gods, and horrific-looking devilish creatures flying in between the description of the movie; and on the front a man and woman embracing in front of a massive, multi-headed dragon. It was exactly the type of movie to catch the attention of a little boy perusing movie shelves on a Friday night.

Understanding nothing of Greek mythology, I reveled in the action, which was coupled perfectly with a striking musical score. I remember each adventure of Jason and his Argonauts in the detail of strong childhood impressions: from their struggle to escape the bronze colossus come to life, to trapping Harpies with nets, to eventually stealing the Golden Fleece from under the nose(s) of the Hydra and battling it out with an army of skeletons. I remember especially the Fleece itself, shimmering in the dark, with its power to bring the dead back to life (most notably reviving the beautiful Nancy Kovack who played Medea).

Okay, aside from waxing nostalgic over my childhood, why bother bringing up a sixty-year-old film and the mythical events it immortalized in the mind of a small child? We believe Jason's quest carries with it many parallels to the journey of a mixed martial artist, most especially for those who practice Brazilian Jiu Jitsu. Like the voyage of Homer's Odysseus, the perils of the journey define the life of the hero, and carry with it far more than mere adventure, offering for the reader a metaphorical understanding of the struggles of their own lives. Let's take a more in-depth look at the myth and its modern parallels.

Without going into too much detail about the political background to Jason's story, the gist of the journey's beginnings is this: King Pelias, who has stolen the throne which rightfully belongs to Jason, orders him to retrieve the legendary Golden Fleece located at the end of the known world, in Colchis (a city on the Black Sea, near modern Georgia). Jason begins preparations for the quest, holding a series of games to determine which heroes will join him on his ship, the Argo, taking only the best the Greek world had to offer, including Hercules, the twins Castor and Polydeuces, and the poet Orpheus. Along the way, as the movie represented quasi-accurately, they encounter various trials: a tribe of murderous, six-armed giants, a flock of Harpies, the Clashing Rocks, and of course the Hydra which guarded the Fleece itself. Eventually the heroes claim the fleece (not without a number of losses among the crew), and sail back home. While other heroes like Hercules and Theseus go to the

Underworld and return, thus "triumphing" over Death, Jason undertakes a voyage to the unknown and deadly realm of Colchis, which stands in for the Underworld. The trope of the "Hero's Journey" is nothing new, but humor me a moment while I break down its particularly striking similarities to our own wild experiences on the mats.[44]

Put yourself in the shoes of Jason, the central character of the story, as you begin your journey in combat sports. Like the titular hero, we start in the ineptitude of inexperience, called to greatness but largely unable to fulfill that calling without the help of our crew, our guides, and the many struggles in store. The crew of heroes are our gym-mates, equally unprepared but at our side and willing to face the uncertain future with us; our guides are the gods, without whose help we would have perished immediately and spectacularly, and with whose wisdom we learn to navigate the perils ahead. The metaphorical "perils" here might seem obvious enough, but can include (though they are not limited to): our many injuries, our ego, the strength and character of our rivals, mastering techniques, improving our conditioning, and competing in our first tournaments. But it's not just in the generalities where we might find parallels, but the particulars of the Argonauts' journey hold special significance. For instance, the prevalence of winged, multi-limbed, or multi-headed monsters is worth brief treatment here.

After briefly showing off their athletic abilities in games staged after their arrival on the island of Lemnos, the Argonauts land in the territory ruled by King Cyzicus of the Doliones. The first monstrous creatures the Argonauts encounter are the six-armed Gegeneis, a violent and savage race of "earth-born" giants who attack them. As the poet Apollonius of Rhodes describes them in his account of Jason's voyage, "each had six massive hands, two from his sturdy shoulders, and four below, attached to his terrible sides."[45] The nature of the creatures is important as they stem from the Earth (Ge or Gaia), who spawns various multi-limbed challengers to Zeus and the Olympians, but their physiology is even more important, especially in regard to athletic metaphors of domination. If you're like me, a thoroughly average striker, you've taken your fair share of beatings in sparring rounds with professionals. Encountering these high-level strikers first-hand is like encountering a six-armed monster—the blows land hard and fast and seemingly from every direction until the best you can do is turtle up in defense and try to weather the storm until the end of the round. Equally so, when pitted against a superior grappler, it can feel as if they somehow have extra limbs, the dominating effect is so thorough and merciless. The monsters the heroes encounter at the beginning of their journey are representative of the first leg of one's journey in combat sports—when one is woefully unprepared for the skill level of one's opponents, and it feels as if the entire gym is inhabited by Gegeneis.

In the myth, they rush down from the mountain and lay a trap for the Argonauts, but Hercules takes the lead in slaughtering them with his bow until the rest arrive and fight until they finally manage to kill them all. Their corpses lie like hewn tree trunks along the sea-shore, some with their heads and chests in the water, others with their feet in the sea. Thus, in the words of the poet, "the contest (*aethlos*) was ended without fear." Well, not quite. The myth includes the detail that after the Argonauts feasted with the Doliones they sailed away, only to be blown off course at nightfall and ending up where they started. But this time, the Doliones thought they were enemies and attacked them, led by Cyzicus whom Jason kills. Friends—enemies—frenemies?

The next significant encounter is in the land of the Bebryces. In a motif we have seen before with Theseus, no visitor is allowed to depart and continue on their way without fighting King Amycus, son of Poseidon, in a boxing match. He is depicted as a braggart and a bully and Polydeuces (whose father is Zeus) takes him on— Castor and Polydeuces are famed as horsemen and boxers and were patrons of athletes and athletic contests. It is agreed that the winner can do whatever he likes with the loser; in one version, Polydeuces gives Amycus such a beating that he surrenders and is made to promise that he will stop abusing travelers. In another, he actually kills Amycus and there is a battle between the Argonauts and the Bebryces which the Argonauts of course win.

The heroes labor next to rescue the blind Phineus, relegated to exile on an island where Harpies—half-human, half-bird—steal his food (or befoul it) every day. Their name comes from a Greek word meaning "to snatch" or "to grab" and they have been sent as a punishment by the gods for reasons which vary according to which of the ancient sources you choose. Jason and his Argonauts drive away (or kill) the Harpies and free the old man in return for his counsel concerning the location of their destination Colchis. Not necessarily multi-limbed, the Harpies nevertheless represent a different kind of challenge, arguably even more daunting than that of the Gegeneis. An aerial enemy, the Harpies inhabit a new medium, and as such require a unique approach to killing them. They have sharp beaks and talons and the Argonauts (in the film at least) have to use a net to trap them. Likewise, as one progresses on the mats, new challenges, new visitors, new obstacles present themselves, requiring the burgeoning martial artist to adapt or die (so to speak). Practical examples abound, but I'll use one from personal experience.

My first gym was strictly combat-based. We were forbidden to drill or spar using any techniques but the ones which could be applicable in a real-life combat scenario. As such, we were never exposed to the variety of open guards available to sport Jiu Jitsu players, nor were we given the opportunity to learn leg-locks. When I left that gym, I encountered gym mates who didn't play by those rules; who sat guard, rolled for my legs, or practiced other equally bewildering strategies. If I wanted to continue learning Jiu Jitsu, I had to adapt to this new world I'd been thrust into. I had to adapt to a new opponent.

Having bested all obstacles, and having lost a number of his crew along the way (a metaphor in itself, as I've lost count of how many of my buddies in the gym have stopped training altogether), the ultimate challenge then, for Jason, is the Golden Fleece—the culmination of all his (and his crews') strivings—which is here represented by the near-mythical Brazilian Jiu Jitsu black belt. Guarding the Fleece is an equally "ultimate" enemy, the "final boss" so to speak—the Hydra. In the movie version (which I like better, for purposes of metaphor) Jason slays the beast, but in the actual mythology Jason is provided with a sleeping potion by Medea, and after the beast has fallen asleep he sneaks past it and steals the Fleece. Regardless of the means by which Jason conquers the Hydra, what exactly does this challenge represent? As the ultimate task, it can be a metaphor for any number of "tasks" needed to earn one's black belt: time (ten years, on average), number of opponents, competitions, injuries, etc. I think perhaps it's best understood as a significant mile-marker along the way, which for me (even though I haven't yet earned my black belt) was winning a bronze medal at the Nogi World Championship. While it may seem minor, having only competed up to that point in smaller local tournaments, entering "on the world's stage" so to speak, represented a significant departure in my Jiu Jitsu journey from what I believed I was previously capable of. It was my Hydra, which one way or another needed dealing with. The Hydra is Hercules' serpentine opponent, with regenerating heads—so, like a scary combat opponent who keeps coming back for more or with new tricks, with new heads venomously attacking. In the myth, the Fleece is guarded by a giant snake; in the film it becomes the "Hydra", but it's actually the battle with the "children of the Hydra's teeth"—skeletal soldiers who keep regenerating—which echoes the Herculean Hydra more accurately in this scene.

While there are significant metaphorical implications implicit in both versions of the story, I am inclined to appreciate the original mythology more than Hollywood's iteration. Truer to our own experience, no man or woman is an island in martial arts, and the fact that Jason needed the aid of Medea in order to secure the Fleece is indicative of the help we all require in order to earn out black belt. In fact, the task would be impossible without significant help, both from our respective Medeas, as well as our loyal crew.

Finally, we come to the Golden Fleece itself. Originally a symbol of royal authority (hence the reason why Jason sought it, as he was trying to reclaim his rightful kingship), it was also held to possess a number of magical powers. Prominent among them was the ability to heal (and the name Jason actually means "healer" in Greek). The obvious metaphorical significance of the Fleece's royal symbolism in relation to a Jiu Jitsu black belt, is, well, obvious, but less so are its regenerative qualities. A black belt is a symbol of destruction, no doubt, as anyone who has rolled with one can attest, but perhaps of less consideration is its ability to heal its wearer, as well as those who come into contact with them. The physical, social, and psychological benefits of Jiu Jitsu can't be overstated—it's a sport where we play at killing one another, but equally so it is one in which we find community and self-respect.[46] Regardless of whether we are Jason or one of the Argonauts, if we maintain our place on the ship we will be changed for the better. We will overcome the Gegeneis, the Harpies, and the Hydra, and return home with the riches of our spoil.[47]

THE AGE OF BARBARIANS IS OVER

A staple of my teenage physical education was the occasional locker-room conversations about which UFC fighter was the most dominant at that moment. Knowing nothing about combat sports (except that it involved the occasional crowd-adored brutal knock out), these conversations inhabited the periphery of my mind, yet they're memories which stick with me, especially now that I've been training for many years.

And who were these mythical bruisers of my adolescent imagination? There was Jacob "Tito" Ortiz, Chuck "The Iceman" Liddell, and perhaps most famously (though interestingly the least talented, never holding a UFC championship belt) Kevin Ferguson A.K.A. Kimbo Slice. It's no surprise given the nature of his rise to fame (from backyard brawling to the UFC Octagon), as well as his physical prowess and intimidating demeanor, that Kimbo Slice would be the biggest object of fascination for this group of sixteen-year-old boys. In fact, within a circle of particularly rowdy athletes I knew, his backyard brawling antics inspired their own version in parking lots throughout our suburban neighborhoods. I was never witness to these spectacles (assuming they were more than rumor), but considering there were no combat sports gyms in the Charleston area at the time, it's safe to assume the level of skill involved was little less than Kimbo's own close-quarter slugging strategy.

Still though, with the exception of the Tae-Kwan-Do or Kenpo dojo, our only exposure to fighting were these heavy-handed heroes, battering each other with little more than their massive fists in a sport where all forms of martial arts were permitted. And that, coupled with a generally western, xenophobic bias towards hand-to-hand fighting (rather than the more "cowardly" ground techniques of eastern countries), left us with few influential alternatives. The barbarians were at the gates, and they put on a hell of a show.

Considering the Ultimate Fighting Championship was founded by members of the Gracie family in order to prove the superiority of Brazilian Jiu Jitsu over other forms of combat, it's surprising that after the original dominance of Royce Gracie had subsided, hordes of American bruisers spilled over into the Octagon, battering opponents and captivating audiences for years to come until the equalizing influence of Jiu Jitsu had been disseminated into the American culture. Besides the aforementioned veteran brawlers, one in particular is worth mentioning in conjunction with the spectacles of antiquity, in particular those of the Roman Colosseum.

In May 2001, a seventeen-year-old Robbie Lawler exploded onto the combat sports scene with a string of spectacular knock-outs (thirteen of his first twenty fights). Known and feared for his ferocity and seeming invincibility on the feet, the then sparsely tattooed Lawler soon covered over his left shoulder and bicep with a picture of a victorious gladiator, sword in hand and leering through his helmet, the ruins of the Colosseum close in the background. For Lawler, a staple of the old guard of UFC brawlers, to have a gladiator etched on his shoulder is precisely indicative of the kind of fighting expected from early UFC events—brutal, bloody, and standing toe-to-toe with one's opponent. Interesting too to note that many of the gladiators in the Roman arena were viewed by the spectators as literal "barbarians," the foreignness of the combat an added spectacle for the Roman onlookers.

In contrast to the Greek palaestra, where male citizens trained and competed with their neighbors (mostly in the grappling arts), stands the Roman arena, with its legions of foreign gladiators, trained in armed stand-up fighting. Largely bloodless, and arguably more complex, the Greek-based grappling discipline offered audiences a more civilized alternative to the bloodier exchanges of a purely striking-based discipline. Likewise today, the growing prevalence of Brazilian Jiu Jitsu in the realm of televised combat sports has led to a technically superior fighting style, decreasing the need for opponents to batter one another senseless (though the demand for bloody spectacle persists). One finds fewer examples of the pure bruiser in contemporary combat culture, which is increasingly dominated by technically superior fighters. The age of barbarians is over.

But what's next? Especially for those of us who are growing older—older, at least, in the premature miles a combat sport will tack on to a perfectly young and healthy body—in the sport where, like any sport, the young with new ideas and fresh legs to stand on (usually) prevail in the contest? What's next for those of us who secretly long for just a smattering of the barbarian days, or who have a bit of the barbarian still left in them?

We, like the barbarians still hanging around on the fringes of the sport, still have our place, and even those now who seem at the cutting edge of competitive achievement (the Cole Abates, the Ruotolos) will be replaced in turn. The nature of the palaestra is change. To greater or lesser degrees, and usually for the better. I believe this is because the nature of our humanity is to grow, explore, expand, and create, and the palaestra, both as a Greek institution and as a contemporary phenomenon, is uniquely suited as a gathering place for people most likely to bring about innovations in sport and culture.

And we are uniquely suited in our current moment to observe and contribute to both arts and athletics, especially as they coalesce in our Jiu Jitsu and combat sports gyms. As I reflect on the final words in the final chapter of this book, pouring out of me in a rush of nostalgia, and thinking of the brown belt I've only recently received after nearly eight years of growing in the sport I love, I can only be grateful that I live in a time when the spirit of the original palaestra is flourishing all over the world—when I can visit a gym in London, in Philadelphia, in Denver, in San Diego, or in Boone, NC, roll to the death with complete strangers, and afterward talk about any and everything from politics, to medicine, to philosophy, and of course, to the numberless vulgar topics that flourish when a bunch of us get together. The

Greeks gave the world the palaestra as an example of the ways in which a person might strive for excellence in all disciplines, be they artistic or athletic, and it's my hope that the original spirit of those ancient places will continue to enliven us in the years to come.

BIBLIOGRAPHY

Ancient Authors are generally available in several translations, especially those in the *Loeb Classical Library Collection* from Harvard University Press. Many important passages dealing with Greek combat sports and Philostratus' *Gymnastike* are included in Stocking and Stephens' book of sources. For myths, the fullest accounts are to be found in Gantz's collection.

Eadie, Rod. 2023. "An Overview of Contemporary Scientific Research into the Physiological and Cognitive Benefits of Judo Practice." *Martial Arts Studies*, 14.78-82.

Gantz, Timothy. 1996. *Early Greek Myth. A Guide to Literary and Artistic Sources*. 2 volumes. Johns Hopkins University Press.

Hawhee, Debra. 2004. *Bodily Arts: Rhetoric and Athletics in Ancient Greece*. University of Texas Press.

Larmour, David H. J. 1999. *Stage and Stadium: Drama and Athletics in Ancient Greece*. Weidmann Press.

Poliakoff, Michael. 1987. *Combat Sports in the Ancient World: Competition, Violence, and Culture*. Yale University Press.

Reid, Heather L. 2011. *Athletics and Philosophy in the Ancient World: Contests of Virtue*. Routledge.

Sansone, David. 1992. *Greek Athletics and the Genesis of Sport*. University of California Press.

Stocking, Charles H., Stephens, Susan A. 2021. *Ancient Greek Athletics. Primary Sources in Translation*. Oxford University Press.

ENDNOTES

1   Poliakoff 1987, 12-18 describes the palaestra; his ground-breaking book *Combat Sports in the Ancient World: Competition, Violence, and Culture* remains the most comprehensive and best-documented study available.

2   Arrichion: Poliakoff 1987, 62-63; Philostratus, *Imagines* 2.6; Milo: Poliakoff 1987, 117-119.

3   Larmour 1999, 26-41

4   Wrestling: Poliakoff 1987, 23-53; Pankration: 54-63; Boxing: 68-88.

5   Poliakoff 1987, 99-103.

6   Aeschylus, *Prometheus Bound*, 389; 756-57; 920; 1019; Sophocles, *Oedipus the King*, 879-881; Larmour 1999, 110-111.

7   Entitled *The Interrelationship of Drama and Athletics in Classical Greece* (University of Illinois 1987).

8   Larmour 1999, 16-17; 24-26. Plato, *Republic* 376E, 522A; *Laws* 795E.

9   Plato, *Republic* 410A-412B.

10 I had better luck with an undergraduate in my Ancient Sports class at Illinois one summer, Mr. Terry Glaudel.

11 Entitled *The Arena of Satire* (University of Oklahoma Press, 2016).

12 Joshua Willms received his black belt in Brazilian Jiu Jitsu under Gabe Hernandez and Team LEAD, and currently coaches the Texas Tech BJJ team. He recently completed a PhD in pharmacology and neuroscience and is in his third year of medical school.

13 The turning-post (and racing in general) are rich in metaphorical possibility: Larmour 1999, 99-108.

14   Philo, a Jewish Philosopher writing in the early years of the Roman Empire draws upon a long tradition of using imagery from combat sports to describe *arete* and virtuous conduct more generally; this passage is aptly cited by Poliakoff (1987, 10) in his opening discussion of the role of endurance, skill, and strength in the Greek combat sports.

15   According to Pausanias 9.22.3: "in the gymnasium there is a painting of her. There she is, Corinna, binding her head with a ribbon to signal the victory she won over Pindar in Thebes with a poem."

16   Pindar *Olympian* 8.65-73; C.A. Wheelright, in *Pindar and Anacreon*. Harper: 1846, p.61.

17   In the Panathenaic festival at Athens, reorganized to rival the four great Panhellenic gatherings, there were prizes for 2nd place in combat events like wrestling and pankration as well as for races and the pentathlon; moreover, prizes were of monetary and other value (e.g, jars of olive oil).

18   *Thumos*: the heart, vital spirit, courage, resolution, endurance, appetite, fury; *menos*: passion, spirit, courage, vigor, strength, power, rage. Cf. *menos antipalon*, "the vigor that wrestles against old age" mentioned above with reference to Alcimedon and his grandfather in Pindar's *Olympian* 8.

19   For a broad discussion of ancient sport as "a ritual sacrifice of energy," see Sansone 1992.

20   For diet and other aspects of Greek athletic training, see the *Gymnastike* by Philostratus. For the depiction of wounds, the so-called Terme Boxer statue provides a good example.

21   The trainer adhered to the rigid Tetrad System, of which Philostratus disapproves (*Gymnastike* 54).
22   Athenaeus 629 B-C; see Larmour 1999, 22-24.
23   Diogenes Laertius, 3.4: on account of his *euexia*, excellent physique, robust figure.
24   Plato, *Apology of Socrates* 30E. He adds that he has been given to the city as a gift from the gods.
25   See Hawhee 2004, 27-43 on athletics and rhetoric, and the "sophist-athlete"; Reid "Wrestling with Socrates," in Reid 2011, 43-55.
26   Pausanias 1.39.3: Theseus beat him at wrestling "mainly by his skill" (*sophia*); up to that point, only size and strength were used in wrestling. Cercyon is said to have invented taking the legs of his opponent; in vase-paintings, Theseus is depicted as holding him in a headlock as he tries to grab the hero's foot, and as holding him in a waist-lock from behind, preparing to hoist him from the ground. See Poliakoff 1987, 37; 42-46; 94; 136-37.
27   A long list of skills based upon the ability to "discern" things (such as the movements of the stars, the rotation of the seasons etc.) and ways of improving day-to-day life, including fire, building shelters, and making tools. See Aeschylus, *Prometheus Bound*, 442-506.
28   Philostratus *Gymnastike*, 16; elsewhere (*Imagines* 2.32) he describes a painting of Palaestra, a maiden described as the daughter of Hermes, surrounded by "earth-born" children depicted in various positions, very likely representing different kinds of wrestling.
29   See Poliakoff 1987, 54-56, who notes that Hercules "employs some remarkably irregular tactics in his struggle against the barbarian ogre."

30   Sostratus (Acrochersites) and Leontiscus: Pausanias 6.4.1-3; Poliakoff 1987, 27-28; 57

31   The Cilician pankratiast, see Philostratus, *Heroicus* 14.4-15.3. Poliakoff (1987, 62) interprets the move as clinging to the heel and not letting go. In *Gymnastike* 36, describing the "big in small" athlete, Philostratus mentions the Cilician wrestler Maron, who could be the same individual.

32   See Sam Harris' 2012 essay "The Pleasures of Drowning" (https://www.samharris.org/blog/the-pleasures-of-drowning): he likens grappling with someone trained in BJJ to "falling into deep water without knowing how to swim" and describes training as "to continually drown—or, rather, to be drowned, in sudden and ingenious ways—and to be taught, again and again, how to swim."

33   Lucian, *Anacharsis* 1-3.

34   Pausanias, 8.40.1-2; Philostratus, *Imagines* 2.6; *Gymnastike* 21.

35   We've included the Greek terms here because they have several possible meanings in English.

36   Pindar, *Isthmian* 4. 45-48. The Greek word *amaurosai* means to diminish, make dim or faint.

37   Pindar, *Isthmian* 4.49-53.

38   Oppian, *Halieutica* 2.43-55; 232-40; 253-320, a long and graphic account of a violent struggle.

39   Plato, *Ion* 541E; cf. *Euthyphro* 15D: "Like Proteus, you must be held until you talk."

40   Homer, *Odyssey* 18.1-125.

41   See the descriptions in Hesiod, *Theogony*, 300-330; 820-870; both are hybrid monsters, Typhon with a hundred snake-heads and Echidna also half-snake (they

also produced the Hydra, whom Hercules destroyed); Chimaera: 319-325; see also Homer, *Iliad* 6.179-184.

42   In this context, it is interesting that the most famous centaur of all, Chiron (or Cheiron), the tutor of boy Achilles (and Jason) in all sorts of skills, has a name derived from the Greek word for "hand" (CHEIR). His father was Apollo, who taught him his arts: medicine, herbs, music, archery, hunting, and prophecy. Sometimes his forelegs are represented as human rather than equine. See Philostratus, *Imagines* 2.2.

43   See our forthcoming study of this and other such depictions, "Grappling with Centaurs."

44   Some incidents are rendered in the movie, others appear in the Greek literary sources and myths about Jason and the Argonauts (see Gantz 1996, 340-373); we have blended these in our account.

45   Apollonius Rhodius, *Argonautica*, 1.941-6; 985-1011.

46   See the useful review article by Eadie 2023.

47   A final figure of interest is Talos, a boulder-throwing colossus whom the crew encounter on the island of Crete. Forged by Hephaestus, this mysterious giant has only one point of weakness, an exposed vein in his ankle. Bewitched by Medea, scrapes his ankle on a rock and the ichor (divine version of blood) flows out and he crashes to the ground, dead.

About Candle Light Press

Candle Light Press exists to publish diverse and original works in both graphic and text formats. Our purpose is to help unique voices persist in the world. We are proud to present our inaugural CLP Classical work, *AGONY*, by Joshua Kulseth and David Larmour.

www.candlelightpress.com

CLASSICAL

candle light press™   1470 Walker Way, Coralville, IA 52241
ding@candlelightpress.com

www.ingramcontent.com/pod-product-compliance
Lightning Source LLC
Chambersburg PA
CBHW040624240426
43666CB00020BA/2915